THREE

SIMPLE

STEPS

A MAP TO SUCCESS IN BUSINESS AND LIFE

THREE

SIMPLE

STEPS

BENBELLA

BenBella Books, Inc.
Dallas, Texas

BenBella

BenBella Books, Inc.
10300 N. Central Expressway, Suite 400
Dallas, TX 75231
www.benbellabooks.com
Send feedback to feedback@benbellabooks.com

Printed in the United States of America
10 9 8 7 6 5 4 3 2 1

Library of Congress Cataloging-in-Publication Data is available for this title.
ISBN 978-1-936661-71-8

Editing by Erin Kelley
Copyediting by Deb Kirkby
Proofreading by Brittany Dowdle and Cape Cod Compositors, Inc.
Cover design by Jason Gabbert
Text design and composition by Neuwirth & Associates, Inc.
Printed by Berryville Graphics

Distributed by Perseus Distribution
perseusdistribution.com

To place orders through Perseus Distribution:
Tel: 800-343-4499
Fax: 800-351-5073
E-mail: orderentry@perseusbooks.com

Significant discounts for bulk sales are available. Please contact
Glenn Yeffeth at glenn@benbellabooks.com or 214-750-3628.

To Audrey, who taught me that even in the darkest moments we can still choose to turn our attention to the sound of songbirds, and to Lynda, who lights up my life every time she steps in the room.

Dear Reader,

I know that life can often feel like you're thrashing around in quicksand. The harder you struggle, the deeper you sink, until you can't see how you'll ever be free. This doesn't have to be your experience. I've taught the principles of the *Three Simple Steps* to individuals and groups for many years, and it has been a joy for me to see the dramatic changes in people's lives. For a long time, many of them have encouraged me to write it all down. So I've written *Three Simple Steps* to show you how to free yourself and become everything you are meant to be.

This book is the real deal. I came from a poor background with as many hang-ups as anyone else. I had no family or business connections to help me get ahead in the world. Honestly, I have no identifiable skill or talent. I have, however, diligently studied the attributes, talents, and insights of self-made men and women.

I observed three common behaviors in them all that helped them break free from the quicksand of their situations. What intrigued me was that even though they went against the common thinking of the time, their behaviors have since been shown to match up with our modern understanding of the laws of energy. *Three Simple Steps* provides a map to success in business and life based on proven laws of physics, and is supported by recent neuroscientific evidence.

I resisted writing this book until I felt as though I could stand up and talk about what it takes to achieve the American dream. When I was younger and not motivated by financial independence, I used these steps to achieve a life of travel and adventure, visiting more than fifty countries while earning a mid-six-figure salary. After I turned forty, I used the same system to achieve financial independence. I started a company with a few thousand dollars, and it sold a few years later for more than $100 million. Then I did it again in another business field entirely. I am currently building my third company in less than ten years. I'm not bragging or talking myself up; I want you to know the truth, and to trust what I'm going to tell you.

Quality of life means different things to different people. In Western civilization, it is impossible to achieve a higher quality of life without financial resources. Becoming financially successful is at the core of this book. For me, however, the path to financial independence went hand in glove with improvements in all aspects of a balanced life. Our lives are not meant to be a struggle but a joyful trip, and I hope this book can help you realize that.

The number *three* has significance throughout human history. It is the tripartite nature of the world as heaven, earth, and waters, or the three phases of the moon. It is human as body, soul, and spirit. Whether it's the Holy Trinity or the Yin-Yang-Tao, any person can understand and apply a complex concept through an appreciation of three key elements.

Think of a television. It is a complicated piece of technology. You don't have to become expert in the science of fluorescence or plasma technology to understand the three simple actions of the on/off switch, channel button, and volume control in order to have an enjoyable viewing experience. So it is with understanding the concept of success, and all you need do is make three simple changes in your life.

Similarly, this book has three parts, each dedicated to one step, which must be practiced in the order written. Success cannot be achieved by changing the order or by skipping a step. The first step is to escape the quicksand by reclaiming your individual mentality. The second step empowers you to create those moments of insight that separate the successful from the rest. The third step shows you how to turn your ideas into your new experiences.

I'm hoping this book will really speak to a few of you in particular. I was a road warrior for many years, spending more time in airports than my home. I know the feeling of racing around while trying to convince yourself that what you are doing actually counts for something. But I remember how I felt while I was living that life; there was a gnawing in my solar plexus reminding me that I was born to make more of my life . . . to make a difference. That feeling of wanting to control our own destinies, but not knowing how, is what I call "the quicksand feeling." Psychology teaches that men value respect over love, and we want to look back on our lives with a measure of pride that we achieved something worthwhile.

In sharing my three simple steps, I have also met many women who sacrificed their aspirations to raise and nurture a family. As the family members find their own paths away from the home, these wives and mothers can suffer from a very real sense of grief. They often speak of a lack of confidence when returning to a work environment that has changed drastically in the intervening years, especially in terms of technology. Today, however, being fifty years old feels like thirty used to, and there is a whole new adventure awaiting anyone brave enough to try. You just need to know how to get it started.

This book is also a rallying cry. Every week, I meet people who are desperate to be in charge of their own futures, but they can't come up with an idea to help them get started. Others have an idea but then spend thirty minutes telling me why now is the wrong time to start it.

There is never a wrong time to take control of your life. There have been thirty-two major recessions in the United States since 1850. In each one, household names like General Electric (US economy collapse and run on gold) and Microsoft (stagflation) started off as small businesses. In fact, sixteen of the thirty companies that make up the Dow Jones Industrial Average were started during a recession. These include Procter & Gamble, Disney, Alcoa, McDonald's, and Johnson & Johnson. After every recession, there is an upsurge in the pioneering spirit that is unique to America. The 2001–2003 recession period saw the number of personal businesses grow from 16.9 to 18.6 million, and I started my first company right in the middle of it. History shows there is never a bad time to reinvent yourself. Don't get left behind.

If you check Amazon.com, you'll find more than nine thousand titles in the category of *self-help success*. Many of them offer a helping hand, but the choice is overwhelming: the thirteen paths to . . . the forty-eight laws of . . . When all you want is to improve your quality of life, how are you supposed to learn forty-eight laws about anything before the quicksand pulls you under?

Some self-help book authors have sizeable egos. You can often identify these by the coiffed head with scary white teeth that leers at you from the cover. The pages read like Sunday sermons full of queasy quotations taken out of context. Puking parables exhort you to staple a resignation letter to your boss's head and buy a one-way ticket to Tibet. As valuable as their information might be, it can't be digested without a bottle of antacids in hand. This book will show you how to get out of the quicksand . . . without inducing indigestion.

The most popular books in the self-help category were either written almost a century ago or based on ideas from that era, when our culture and society were very different. It was an even more male-dominated world, and the basic laws of physics that we all take for granted today had not been generally accepted. Most of the authors, both back then and more recently, did not achieve the success they were preaching about until after their books started to sell well. It is dubious information, to say the least.

This book *is* the real deal. I have all the money I need, and all profits I receive from this book will go directly to cancer treatment research and development. I am also donating a free copy to every library in the United States for reasons you'll discover in the story. *Three Simple Steps* is a map to success in business and life. Though I am normally an intensely private man, at the behest of my publisher, I have illustrated the steps with authentic personal stories that show how an ordinary life is made extraordinary by doing nothing more than applying these principles. In return, I ask only that you share your own success stories from implementing the *Three Simple Steps* in your life at www. threesimplesteps.com.

Let's get started.

Cheers,

Trevor Blake

CONTENTS

PART ONE

ESCAPING THE QUICKSAND

Reclaiming Your Mentality

To see with one's own eyes, to feel and judge without succumbing to the suggestive power of the fashion of the day, to be able to express what one has seen and felt in a trim sentence or even in a cunningly wrought word. Is that not glorious? Is it not a proper subject for congratulation?

ALBERT EINSTEIN, 1934

RARE IS THE PERSON who becomes rich working for someone else. Rarer still is the inventor whose ideas get through the scientific peer-review process or the revolutionary artist loved immediately by the critics. How many companies that are household names today were created by a consenting group of people sitting in a meeting room? Companies as diverse as Disney, Mattel, and Apple started in a home garage and were driven by the inspiration of just one or two people.

Being successful in anything requires a high degree of individualism. Individualism requires control of mentality. I'm not going to insist that you can change yourself with positive thinking; that can help you feel better about the life you have, but ultimately what you want is a better life. That's what I'm going to help you with.

Reclaiming your mentality is about becoming the person you were born to be—an individual with the power to think for yourself and with an unlimited potential to achieve great things. Getting out of the quicksand of your life means you must recognize yourself as one among the flock, and win back your identity through control of mentality. It can be the difference between life and death.

1

A Matter of Life and Death

BY 1970, THE DOCTORS called Audrey a walking miracle. She called herself "one of God's little works in progress." Born in 1929, in Liverpool, England, a decade before World War II demolished half the city, she was always a pretty, petite girl, with black, wavy hair. Although Liverpool was a blue-collar working city, her family enjoyed a middle-class lifestyle, and Audrey was the apple of her father's eye.

At the outbreak of the war, she refused to join the thousands of women and children who were evacuated to the countryside. Instead, her father dug an air-raid shelter at the end of their small garden. Because of its strategic importance to the war effort, Liverpool was the most heavily bombed city in England aside from London. Every night from September 1940 through the final German blitz in January 1942, the family huddled in their damp shelter as the world above them shuddered.

Audrey's neighbors were some of the four thousand lives lost. However, her home survived two direct hits from incendiary bombs. The family escaped physical injury, but her mother's nerves were shattered. While her father continued his risky engineering work at the port, Audrey took over running the household.

Although life remained tough in the late war years, the family returned to a normal routine. Each evening when the clock on the mantelpiece chimed six o'clock, Audrey made a mug of fresh tea and hurried to the garden gate to greet her father as he returned from work. One sunny evening as she waited for him to appear round the corner at the end of the street, a huge explosion rocked the sidewalk. She watched as a fireball rose into the sky above the port. The mug slipped from her hand and as it smashed on the floor she knew intuitively it was bad news.

A munitions ship in the harbor had exploded just as everyone was heading home. Audrey's father survived the initial blast, but eventually died from his wounds.

Well-meaning friends and relatives wanted to put Audrey and her brother into care and her mother into a rest home. Audrey fought them all to keep her family together. With no income coming into the household, a younger brother to look after, and a mother who had withdrawn from the world, she left school at thirteen years of age and made money by scrubbing the steps of the wealthy. Her bubbly personality and the cheeky sense of humor she inherited from her father endeared her to her customers. Soon she was trusted to do their laundry and housework. At sixteen, she took a job in a factory.

After several years, with her mother recovering and the war behind them, Audrey was promoted to a supervisory role. She had enough income to start a savings account and plucked up the courage to go to a bank. In a time when a bank manager was as revered as a doctor in the community, this took nerve for a young woman.

Observing her discomfort, a young bank teller came to her aid, completed the paperwork, and helped her open an account. Chatting nervously, Audrey realized they had been at adjoining schools before the war. She agreed to meet him for afternoon tea the following weekend. Two years later, they married.

The bank teller, Harry, was a restless man. Having completed his conscripted service in the Royal Air Force, he found it difficult to adjust to a regular working schedule. He left the bank and tried his hand at several businesses. Friends and relatives criticized the couple. There was a postwar recession in the country. Work was hard to find, and in the views of others, Harry had turned his back on job security. People thought they had lost their senses and were not shy about saying so.

Although the criticism angered Harry, Audrey ignored it in the same way she had ignored those who told her a thirteen-year-old girl could not keep a family together. Literally barefoot and pregnant, she was at Harry's side as they sold fruit and vegetables from a market stall. The business started well, but they expanded too quickly, renting a larger stall and purchasing a bigger van. When the operation failed, Harry, a reasonable handyman, turned to making coffee tables and ottomans for wholesale trade, and Audrey learned how to wield a drill.

By 1962, they had three hungry children to feed, and the debts were piling up. An eviction notice arrived. They rented a shop next to a railway crossing and lived in the three rooms above it. The shop was named after the three children, but it was in a poor part of town where the locals could not afford Harry's furniture. More debts came due, and another eviction notice arrived.

They bundled their three children and all their belongings into an old truck and escaped the city. This only increased the volume of criticism the young couple received from everyone they knew, especially their parents. When the children questioned why everyone was angry with Dad, Audrey brushed it aside. "They just envy our freedom," she told them. "Life is an adventure. Who knows what tomorrow will bring?"

The truck coughed and spluttered through the countryside until it choked to a stop in a small village, deep in the Welsh countryside. Locals pointed out a vacant but derelict farm-house. Hardly daring to believe their luck in finding tenants, the owners accepted a meager monthly rent.

Built in 1601, it had the original boulder walls and black slate floors. The windows were cracked and the roof needed serious repair. A breeze howled through rotted window frames and coated everything with ancient plaster dust. Ever the optimist, Audrey told her family they had found a bargain. She set every-one to work turning it into a home, and somehow managed to feed the family from pots hung over a wood fire.

Leaving the confines of the inner city for the open space of the countryside was like entering the pages of *The Chronicles of Narnia* for the children. Harry found a regular job as a meat truck driver. Audrey made fast friends in the village. Life for the family was on the upswing, but the criticism in letters or over the phone never let up.

Having lived in Liverpool her whole life, Audrey thrived in the clean air and open countryside. A lover of animals, she had soon filled the farmhouse with stray lambs, rabbits, cats, and two old donkeys who wandered up the lane one day. With wild ber-ries, herbs, and elderflowers in abundance, the larder was stocked with homemade jellies and chutneys. The children ate apples and plums off the trees and became adept at growing vegetables.

In the winter of 1969, while having a stand-up wash in icy wa-ter, Audrey found "a few lumps and bumps." After a period of hospital visits, the family doctor warned Audrey she had ad-vanced breast cancer and had less than six months to live.

In those days, the pronouncements of a doctor were like voo-doo curses. If he said you were going to die, people accepted it. Mention of the nearest cancer hospital brought sharp intakes of breath. "She'll go in upright and come out horizontal" was the general sentiment of the villagers. The word *cancer* was only muttered under the breath, and many of the isolated villagers feared it was contagious. When they saw Audrey walking down a lane, people changed direction, and the ignorant pointed. No one wanted to befriend a woman with a death sentence.

The main cause of these habitual reactions was unprecedented media coverage of cancer deaths in the 1960s. People who had worked in the shipyards had been exposed to asbestos for decades. In Liverpool, everyone knew someone who had died of lung cancer. Smoking was still fashionable, and now stars of stage and screen were making mournful headlines. Adding drama to the fear, stories of children fighting leukemia, previously absent from the news, started to feature prominently in the national press.

Audrey and Harry agreed to keep the news secret from the children. Unable to handle the burden, Harry told his oldest child, a daughter, and admonished her to keep it to herself. Within an hour, she told the older of her two brothers, and that night he whispered it to the youngest.

A dark cloud descended over the previously happy household, but Audrey refused to accept that she only had a few months to live. She considered it not as a threat to her own existence but to that of her three children. What stronger power exists than that of a mother protecting her young?

She told anyone who cared to listen that nothing was going to stop her from living long enough to see all three of her children grow up and safely leave her nest. She refused to match the gloomy expressions around her. She berated relatives for their lack of fighting spirit. She walked to the village shop every day until the locals stopped treating her like a leper. She even refused to let the reverend include her name in prayers at Sunday service. She refused to react in the way other people expected.

Seeing the frightened faces of her children, she called a family meeting. She told them, "No one tells me when to die. I decide that, and I alone. I am not leaving until I am good and ready. If any of you try using this as an excuse to skip homework or feel sorry for yourselves, you'll have me to answer to." Seeing such steely determination, no one dared argue.

One day, the middle child spied her through a half-closed door when she was alone in the kitchen. She grimaced in pain, dropped a dish she was washing, and rubbed her chest. Sighing, she looked out of the small window up to a gray sky. As if admonishing a naughty child, she wagged her finger at the clouds. "If you think I'm leaving now to come see you when they're not even grown, you've got another think coming! I am not done here yet. When I am ready to leave, I will let you know. Until then I have work to do."

Audrey confounded the medical experts when she made a rapid recovery from a mastectomy operation, followed by several courses of chemotherapy and radiotherapy. The hospital staff liked her because she always had a smile and a joke to offer. She was genuinely interested in them. She knew all about their love lives, their families, and their birthdays.

Despite having a worse prognosis than many of the people around her, she encouraged other patients to be positive. "What if we are going to die?" she would ask. "At least enjoy those candies your visitor brought in. No one on their deathbed was ever heard to mutter that they were glad they left that last chocolate in the box!"

When she lost her hair as a side effect of the chemotherapy, she had everyone in the hospital try on the wigs that were offered. When even the stiffest of the oncologists completed his ward round with blonde pigtails dangling down his back, the place was in an uproar. When Audrey's natural hair returned, it was completely gray, and she cried for the first and only time.

She saw that some of the other patients did not get many visitors, and the hospital food was limited. At home, the kitchen was turned into a bakery, and the children were taught all the necessary skills. She taught them to cook, and supervised as they took turns making the Sunday roast dinner for the family. Subtly, while providing better food for the lonelier patients, Audrey had ensured her children could take care of themselves. Perhaps because they were enjoying the cookies she always handed out in the outpatient clinic, the doctors extended her life sentence to three years.

Just as things were improving, she suffered another form of cancer, and it was like receiving a second death sentence, even while the first was being served. More operations and treatments prodded at her spirit, and different doctors confirmed that she really did only have a few months left to live. She told them they had it wrong the first time, and this would be no different.

At the same time, Harry lost his job. Work was scarce, and after a few months of trying to find alternatives, he gave up looking altogether. With welfare support limited, Audrey found a part-time position, serving behind the counter of a busy delicatessen in the nearest town. The money was not great, but she was able to bring home leftover meats, pâté, bread, and cheese for the family. She developed a network of relationships with other shopkeepers, and enjoyed interacting with customers. She said it gave her something to take her mind off herself.

The country was in a deep recession, and the government had slowed production down by enforcing a three-day working week for manufacturing. Everyone endured rolling electric blackouts in the winter of 1974. For Audrey's family, this was not an issue. Their utilities were often severed due to nonpayment, so they had learned to cook just as well on an open fire. With the food network Audrey had established in town for leftover cuts from the butcher's shop, and expired food items from the bakers, the family ate better than most. Despite her illness and circumstances, she let nothing get in the way of caring for her children.

The cancer spread to the bones in her spine and femurs. When she could not get a ride into town, she walked the five miles to and from work every day. It was a tough walk for a fit person, but it was a test of endurance for a woman using a stick to disguise a limp.

Despite the pain, she enjoyed being with nature. Whenever school was out, one or more of her children would keep her company.

As her movement deteriorated, some customers could be rude when she took a long time to complete their order in the shop. She would throw out a joke like "I should take less gin with my cornflakes in the morning" and not let anyone's bad manners make her focus on the disability.

She built up a loyal clientele at the shop, and business was never better for the owners, who were now regular visitors to the farmhouse. After school, her children would visit the shop, and help out with chores. In many ways, the shop became an extension of home . . . only warmer!

The doctors gave up predicting her demise. When they told her how ill she was supposed to feel, she would shush them with a wave of her hand. It became like a game. Whenever someone told her something bad or tried to show empathy, she developed the knack of deflecting it with a joke. Then she would reach for a better thought, as if being positive deleted the negativity of others.

In 1978, Audrey's daughter joined the police force, fell in love with a colleague, and married within a year. Just nineteen, the newlyweds found jobs and a home just a short drive away from the family, so they could visit easily. The youngest child joined the Royal Air Force. After finishing basic training, he took a position that allowed him to be home every weekend.

The middle son joined the Royal Navy College. Audrey was intensely proud because working-class children rarely qualified for the officer training. One day, she asked God for an extra favor. She had agreed to stay alive long enough to see her children fly the nest safely, which technically they had all done. Now she decided she wanted to see her son graduate as an officer.

In 1980 and 1981, Audrey needed several more courses of chemotherapy and two operations to repair her deteriorating bones. The pain medicine turned her physical features into those of an elderly woman, but her spirit and sense of humor were untouched.

Despite the discomfort of a 300-mile trip in a vehicle that was falling to bits, Harry and Audrey traveled to their son's graduation. The Queen Mother was the guest of honor. With her legs invaded by cancer, Audrey still managed a perfect curtsey. Audrey knew now she could leave in peace, but she had one more task to complete.

The newly minted naval officer took compassionate leave to return home with his parents. Audrey was failing and needed weekly trips to the hospital for pain medicine and chemotherapy. He took his turn taking her for the treatments.

At the hospital, they were met by Audrey's favorite nurse. The son watched as they greeted each other with bear hugs and exchanged jokes. For the son, it was love at first sight.

Audrey died before their wedding ceremony. She insisted on dying at home in the derelict farmhouse she had come to love. A bed was moved downstairs to the lounge, and the family took turns living in the one room during her last days.

Sitting next to her on the bed, the naval officer held her hand as she drifted in and out of consciousness. He felt her grip tighten. She opened her eyes, and seemed alert for the first time in days. She smiled and looked over to the window. The

13

age and pain washed away from her features, and she let out a small cry. It was not one of pain but more like that of a little girl in delight.

"Dad!" She shouted. Expecting to see his father entering the room, the son looked up. No one was there. Audrey gestured to the window. "Son, this is my father, your Granddad William. You have never met before, but he knows all about you. Say hello." The son waved at the air. "He says I still owe him a fresh mug of tea." They were her last words that she spoke to him.

The farmhouse was in a village of less than 100 residents, but more than 200 people attended Audrey's funeral in May 1982. The twelfth-century church had never been as full. The family recognized the villagers and some of their friends, but more than half the congregation were strangers to them.

The attendees included some of Audrey's childhood friends from Liverpool. As there had never been any mention of it in her letters, most were under the impression that her illness had been sudden. Several customers from the shop she worked at were there.

At the back of the church sat Mr. Garrad, a hard man who everyone in the village gave a wide berth. His wife had committed suicide many years before, and he raised his three boys on his own. An intensely private man, no one knew much about the family. Fighting to control his emotions, he confessed to Audrey's family that for years she had secretly given him food and clothes for the boys, and had often sneaked down to his house to help with cooking or housework when he was forced to work late. Afterward, he placed fresh wildflowers on her grave every week.

A girl the same age as Audrey's daughter was inconsolable. She explained how her mentally ill father had refused to allow "just a girl" to wear anything but rags to school. She was teased so mercilessly that she played truant. Audrey had secretly taken her daughter's spare set of clothes once a week to the delicatessen where she worked. There she had arranged for the girl to change from the rags before and after school. Now a grown woman, she added, "I owe your mother everything!"

Audrey's body is buried on the brow of a hill at the edge of the graveyard, from where there is an unobstructed view across the fields to the farmhouse.

■ ■ ■

Although Audrey was never rich monetarily, she achieved something far more important in her life. In my personal and business life, I have met few people who so perfectly understood the power of controlling their mentality. If this kind of control can put off death for fourteen years, imagine what else it can do.

2

Master of Mentality

WHAT IS MENTALITY?

AUDREY WAS MY MOTHER, and I am the middle child. Thirty years later, I am still happily married to Audrey's favorite chemotherapy nurse. How my mother reacted to her situation inspired me even at a young age. When I was growing up, she was always telling me to pause before I spoke "to give your reaction time to sort itself out." It was sound advice, and I still try to follow it to this day.

Because she was in control of what she allowed into her mind and then managed her thoughts quietly, she always chose her reaction to anything carefully. I remember being beside her hospital bed when some doctors whispered her prognosis amongst themselves but loud enough for us all to hear. I watched her eyes as she computed what they were saying, and then how she took her time to compose herself before speaking. The way she thought was not as important as the way she reacted to her thoughts. Her reaction changed the outcome for herself and all those with whom she interacted. She gave strength to everyone around the hospital bed and, in so doing, gained some herself.

My abiding memories of my teenage years are not of her chronic pain but of all the laughter in our home, her great cooking, and our stumbling walks in the country. That is because she refused to let things inside and outside her mind dictate how she was supposed to react. She wanted family life to be normal and to complete her duties as mother.

When it comes to battling disease, there is mixed evidence for the power of mind over matter. It is also unfair to give the impression, as some writers do, that because a person chooses not to fight their illness that it makes them weak or wrong. The connection between the body, mind, and spirit is too complex for anyone living currently to comprehend. People have a right to choose their reaction, whether it is to fight or accept. I have, however, worked with cancer patients for more than twenty years. I have seen many of what the doctors described as "walking miracles," and the only difference I was able to detect between them and their fellow patients in almost identical situations was their control of mentality.

My mother used her situation to teach me many things, and she always had a philosophical phrase to throw at me. She told me to take nothing at face value, to seek my own truth, not someone else's version of it. She told me over and over again to look the world in the eye and then I could be anything I wanted to be. Most of all, she taught me that my thoughts and reactions are my own responsibility, and that only I can decide how to feel about anything. "No one can make you *feel* sad or angry," she would admonish. "That is a choice you make for yourself as a reaction to the situation you perceive. You can just as easily choose to ignore or laugh about it."

Even now, I do not have her sense of mentality control, and I often let my emotions rule my head. Every now and then though, I remember her advice, pause a moment, and choose a different reaction. Just those small changes in behavior have completely changed the outcome of my life.

Over the years, I have read dozens of autobiographies of famous men and women who could be considered self-made. At first, I approached their life stories with cynicism. I expected to find a key advantage that they had and that I did not, such as a family connection or a financial helping hand. What I found, however, were mostly disadvantaged people who developed an unshakeable belief in their ability to control their lives. They didn't conform to what the world expected of them. They stood out from the crowd, and when presented with the same challenges as others, chose a different and individual reaction. With their evidence and my mother's coaching I began to change my life.

As a child, I suffered from sectarian bullying, and at one time felt the weight of the world on me. One of the first biographies to inspire me was that of a woman known as Madame C. J. Walker, who was born in 1867 to parents who had been slaves. She started life with almost every disadvantage you could imagine: born on a plantation, orphaned, married at fourteen, then a single mother when her husband abandoned her. She had every excuse needed to talk herself out of her potential for success, and I felt a similar predilection for a life of mediocrity.

For a black female entrepreneur today, the barriers to success are many; back then, they must have seemed insurmountable. In 1865 and 1866, state governments in the South enacted laws designed to regulate the lives of the former slaves. These measures, differing from state to state, were actually revisions of the earlier slave codes that had regulated that institution. Some common elements appeared in many of the codes:

- Race was defined by blood; the presence of any amount of black blood made one black.
- Employment was required of all freedmen/women; violators faced vagrancy charges.

- Freedmen could not assemble without the presence of a white person.
- Freedmen were assumed to be agricultural workers and their duties and hours were tightly regulated.
- Freedmen were not to be taught to read or write.
- Public facilities were segregated.
- Owning of guns, and in some states a knife or fork, was forbidden for freedmen.
- Violators of these laws were subject to being whipped or branded.

From this background, however, an uneducated, persecuted, female daughter of slaves became, according to *The Guinness Book of World Records*, the first female self-made millionaire in America.

I was struck by her unshakeable belief. Just like my mother, she refused to let the outside world determine how she was supposed to think and react to any circumstance. I realized that my perceived hardships were nothing when compared to Madame Walker's.

As a child, I used to play cowboys and Indians, mimicking the atrocious Hollywood twist on history in mock gunfights around our farmhouse with an imitation Colt .45. Many years later, I read Samuel Colt's story. His mother died when he was eleven, and his father's business failed soon after, sending him into despair and the family into poverty. His situation was not so different from mine at a similar age, and I was struck by how he refused to use it as an excuse.

In every biography, I recognized how each person had to become a master of their mentality in order to get out of the quicksand of their life. Key to that control was their ability to think and react as an individual, and not as a group, society, or trend dictated.

Using the same self-control, I have changed my mentality from one of poverty to that of a multimillionaire, and my lifestyle with it. I changed thoughts of expecting to fail to ones of anticipating success. I overcame issues of self-esteem to attract my soul mate. When I was twenty-nine, I also chose to ignore doctors who told me to "get my affairs in order," which was their politically correct way of telling me I was about to die. Two days after surgery, I checked myself out of the hospital, and drove 200 miles to start a new job. The abdominal stitches had me bent double like an impression of the Hunchback of Notre Dame, but as I stumbled around the new office, I claimed it was a soccer injury. That was more than twenty years ago. To escape the feeling of being in quicksand, controlling one's mentality is the first essential step.

I began this part of the book with a quotation from Albert Einstein, one of my heroes. What fascinated me most about Einstein's life were not his many scientific achievements, but his contributions to society. During the last twenty-two years of his life, while J. Edgar Hoover and his FBI conducted a top-secret campaign against him, he was actively and passionately involved in numerous struggles for social justice, especially antiracism or what he called "America's Worst Disease." At the time, Einstein's outspoken support for those attacked by fascism abroad and McCarthyism at home often made front-page news, and he was vilified at every opportunity by a negative public relations campaign orchestrated from Washington.

All this was on top of being condemned by his scientific peers as a lunatic, before technology caught up and his theories were validated. Like Madame C.J. Walker, Samuel Colt, and Audrey, Albert Einstein was a *master of mentality*, and I offer this definition and equation in his honor:

Mentality is defined as a habitual mental attitude that determines how you will interpret and react to situations. The mentality equation has three elements:

- **The situation** (what we see, hear, smell, taste, sense, and what the media or people in our lives can make us feel about any of that),
- **The thought** (triggered by how we are made to feel), and

- **The reaction** (how we choose to discharge the emotional thought).

Situation + Thought = Reaction

The quality of our thoughts is important, and books on positive thinking tend to stop there. It is, however, the next step that determines a path of success or frustration: how we react to what we think. Under normal circumstances, we don't exert any control over what we see and hear from the people around us or through the media. Our thoughts tend to be triggered by an automatic emotional response to what we see and hear. Then we react, and for most people it is habitual.

If you have not managed to control any of the sensory input or the thoughts that they trigger, then you let your reaction be influenced by the situation. You have placed responsibility for your life in the minds, opinions, and influence of the outside stimuli. They tell you that you have six months to live, and you die. They tell you the economy is in free fall and you decide it is the wrong time to start the business of your dreams. They tell you you'll soon qualify for assisted living, so you determine that you are too old to go back to college.

To get out of the quicksand, you have to filter what you allow into your mind so that your decisions belong to you as an individual, and not to the fashion or trend of any group. You must choose your own thoughts and the reactions you have to them. You must become an individual again, something most people have not experienced since birth.

HOW MENTALITY IS FORMED

The moment we are born is the most pure in our entire lives. We have seen and heard nothing. Therefore, we have nothing to contemplate or to react to. We are born an individual, and with unlimited potential. One second later, a well-meaning giant with a hand the size of a spade smacks us on the bottom. It is commonly taught that we don't feel pain in the first two weeks of life, but still it startles us. Because of the rude awakening, and the fact that we realize in the same moment that we are away from the warmth and security of the womb, we react. To our parents, our cry is the greatest sound in the universe (until that first sleepless night at home!).

Most parents do not know the secrets of success, so our newborn state of mentality is unguarded. Like a paper towel soaking up water, we absorb everything we sense in our environment. On the one hand, we learn quickly. On the other, we cannot filter anything. We take in the feelings and moods, the opinions and reactions, of those around us. Our state of mind fills up quickly, and most psychologists agree that our mentalities change very little after the age of five. We quickly cease to be individual as we conform to the family around us.

As we age, we usually develop the same habits, and react the same way to outside stimuli, as those we are associated with, such as our parents, school friends, coworkers, or sports and television idols. We mimic their behavior and take on the same values as the groups to which we now belong. We are attracted and repulsed by similar things. The result is that we continually seek experiences that reinforce our learned group behavior and beliefs.

We are encouraged to be team players in a culture of democracy in which the decision or victory goes to the person with the most votes or highest score. In business, we find ourselves in an endless round of meetings in which consensus is the goal, and the lone dissenter is looked upon as a troublemaker. Our culture today shows little tolerance for the genius or the singular voice or anyone who might react unconventionally. Before long, most people will lose all sense of self.

The American dream, however, was not built by a think tank. The country grew on the backs of pioneers. Individuals, armed with little more than an idea and an unshakeable will to survive, achieved unprecedented success in a fresh, new country.

You might be reading this book on a device invented by Apple Inc., a company that is valued at more than $500 billion today, as I type these words on another of their life-changing inventions. Apple's success is attributed to the pioneering spirit of Steven Paul Jobs.

Steve was put up for adoption just after he was born. His adoptive parents named him and brought him up in California. When he was eleven, Steve simply refused to go back to school because he was bored, and his parents moved him to a different school that offered electronics classes. He never conformed to what the world expected of him. He developed a reputation as a loner and had what his teachers called "an odd way of looking at things." He had issues with some teachers, who could not accept that he did not want to fit in with the class mentality that challenged nothing being taught to them. Like Einstein's teachers thought of him, Jobs's high-school teachers considered him disruptive.

In a 2007 interview with *PC World*, his partner Steve Wozniak revealed that they first met during Wozniak's college years, while Jobs was in high school. "We both had pretty much sort of an independent attitude about things in the world, we were both smart enough to think things up for ourselves and not have followed the common disregard of the day, like counterculture.

Steve was more a part of the counterculture thinking and I was really disclosed to it."

This individualism pattern followed Jobs into the workplace, where his manager at his first company, Atari, considered him "a nightmare to work with." When Jobs and Wozniak developed their idea of a personal computer, both Hewlett-Packard and Atari rejected their idea as ridiculous.

Had Steve Jobs accepted the common opinion that surrounded him, who knows what would have become of him? History shows that he had an unshakeable belief in his own mind.

This individual went on to change the lives of a billion people. Had he conformed to group mentality or peer pressure as a child, we might never have heard of him, and you would not be reading this on your mobile electronic device.

Your time is limited, so don't waste it living someone else's life. Don't be trapped by dogma—which is living with the results of other people's thinking. Don't let the noise of others' opinions drown out your own inner voice. And most important, have the courage to follow your heart and intuition. They somehow already know what you truly want to become. Everything else is secondary.

STEVE JOBS

More than once in my life, I have also been called "a nightmare to work with." I have been told by dozens of people that I had my head in the clouds. Employers have reprimanded me for not toeing the company line. My peer group has ridiculed my lack of experience and unique business models. Yet here I am, a serial entrepreneur, writing this book. I do not dare put myself in the same pioneering bracket as a Madame Walker or a Steve Jobs, but it has been a blast of a trip just the same.

One of the secrets has been to control my mentality. It might all sound as if we either have to become a genius or a spiritual master. We do not. Reclaiming mentality is simple and anyone can do it, starting right now.

RECLAIMING MENTALITY IS SIMPLE

Most people ignore a book's introduction. We pick it off the shelf, form an opinion of the title, read the back cover, and scan a few sentences of chapter one. The process of deciding whether or not to read it takes about eleven seconds. With that in mind, I kept my introduction short. If you skipped it, let me reiterate two key points.

#1. The Power of Three.

The number three has been significant throughout human history. It is the tripartite nature of the world as heaven, earth, and waters or the three phases of the moon. It is human as body, soul, and spirit. Whether it's the Holy Trinity or the Yin-Yang-Tao, any person can understand and apply a concept through an appreciation of three simple steps.

Think of a television. It is a complex thing, but if we understand the three simple steps of the on/off switch, channel button, and volume control, we can all have an enjoyable viewing experience. We don't have to become expert in the science of fluorescence.

So it is with understanding the concept of success. Everything in life can be understood enough to be useful to us when it is broken down into a few key principles. We need neither the

detail nor the expert knowledge to get the benefits from a subject. When it comes to success, I believe you need to understand
only three things.

The smell of a freshly baked loaf of bread excites me. (Well,
different things excite us as we age!) Learning a lot about individual ingredients is useful to a professional chef, but I just like
to eat fresh bread. I don't need to understand the chemistry
that takes place in the oven in order to satisfy my hunger. So too
you don't need to grasp anything deeper than the need to control the inputs into your state of mind in order to pull yourself
out of the quicksand.

After I started my first company, there was not enough money
in the business to justify drawing a wage. I subsidized myself by
doing a couple of consulting projects on the side. For one,
George Rathmann was the company chairman, and in 2002 I
was invited to meet him for an interview. In 1999, here's how
Forbes magazine described George Rathmann:

> George Rathmann is the Bill Gates of biotechnology . . . Like his
> high tech counterpart, Rathmann has an uncanny knack for tim-
> ing: He pinpointed a new industry ripe for rapid growth, one
> that needed both a technologist and an entrepreneur. Like
> Gates, he built the single most prosperous company his industry
> has ever known, the Southern California-based Amgen . . . And
> like Gates, he has become a legend in the process, taking on, at
> times, a godlike aura in the eyes of industry insiders . . .
>
> After only a brief stab at retirement, Rathmann became CEO of
> a second startup, the Bothell, Washington-based biotech company
> Icos. This is where the lives of Rathmann and Gates literally met
> as Gates was convinced to invest in biotech. In 1990 Gates invested
> $5 million in Icos, and in subsequent years invested more than
> $17 million. Icos became the largest biotechnology company in
> Washington before being sold to Eli Lilly for $2.3 billion in 2007.

Over dinner, he grilled me more than I had expected. I wanted to impress him but seemed to be failing. Then his wife arrived as we were selecting desserts. With a twinkle in her eye, she asked, "Has he been giving you a tough time? He said he was going to be hard on you to see what you are made of! I felt sorry for you, so thought I'd rescue you before you get indigestion."

With his cover blown, the interrogation became a general discussion on the secrets to business success. When I was getting into detail about plans for my company's future, he held up his hand to stop me. "You don't know what business you are in until you get into the business!" he said. "Don't get bogged down in the detail. Just get started. The rest works itself out." It is one of the best pieces of business advice I have ever received.

In the same spirit I offer it to you here. I may provide a lot of detail in the three simple steps. Take George Rathmann's advice, and once you get the concept, just apply it without worrying too much about the details of how or why it works.

#2. Change a Little, Change a Lot.

The second piece of good news is that only small changes to mentality are required to make giant improvements in your quality of life. The metaphor I use to understand this is to think about a pool table that is neatly set up for a new game. The solid and striped balls rest in formation at the far end of the table, and have little to no purpose when they are resting. Your intention, however, is to turn the rack of inert balls into something different. The cue is your mentality, and the white ball's movement is the reaction to your thoughts.

The very slightest change in angle between the tip of the cue (mentality) and the surface of the white ball has a vastly different impact on the outcome. Make the wrong angle, as I sometimes do when starting a game, and the white ball flies off the table, while the rack of balls remains untouched. I am left feeling frustrated. If, however, I change the angle of the cue only slightly, the white ball smashes the rack of colored balls all over the table. It is a dramatic difference in outcome from a very small change in the angle of mentality, and the success of it feels fulfilling.

So too it is with changing your quality of life with these principles. Change a little and you can change a lot. In learning to control your mentality, you do not have to wear a purple kaftan and drink herbal tea all day. You simply have to make small, often subtle alterations to the way you think and react.

When you are sitting in front of your bank's lending officer, who is challenging your lack of business experience for the venture you want to start with borrowed money, how you react to the criticism or challenge determines whether you get the loan or not. It sounds obvious, but I have steered clear of investing in dozens of bright ideas simply because the person who was presenting to me reacted defensively or negatively to something I asked. Investors more often invest in the jockey (entrepreneur) than the horse (idea). There is no shortage of horses, but winning jockeys are hard to find.

Like it or not, there is a thing that can be called The Millionaire Mentality. There is a frame of mind which puts an individual a long way ahead on the road to success.

J. PAUL GETTY

THE SUBTLE SECRET TO RECLAIMING MENTALITY

When asked her opinion on a particular conflict, Mother Theresa said, "I am not *against* war. I am *for* peace." In that marvelous statement is the distillation of a dozen subjects from quantum physics to theology, and it is the essence of this first step. If you read the rest of this first step, and grasp nothing more than the meaning of this sentence, you would have enough knowledge to make a big difference in your life.

Yes, it starts to sound like feel-good ideology, but some of the world's most hardened industrialists promoted this mental imperative long before any self-help guru caught on to it. Andrew Carnegie was forced by poverty to seek employment as a bobbin boy in a cotton factory, earning $1.20 a week. He rose to be the world's wealthiest man with a personal fortune equivalent to $7 billion in today's value. He exhorted man (it was a macho world back in the 1850s) "to aspire to individualism, to ignore all that was missing in his environment, and to seek only improvement in *what he wants.*"

We must change our thoughts from being *against* things we don't want to being *for* things we do want. It is that simple, just like I promised it would be. That is the subtle change in angle of the cue to the ball, and the outcome will astound you. It is, however, far from easy because it is a lifelong lifestyle change. To introduce that small change in our lives with consistency so that it becomes habitual, we first need to understand some of the key properties of thoughts and words. Understanding these properties will allow you to be more mindful and skillful in handling your mentality in critical situations.

Properties of Thoughts

Many teachers of success theory base their philosophies on the premise that everything in life begins with a thought. They miss a key part of the creative process. *Nothing* is what comes first. Everything starts from nothing, including a thought. This may sound odd coming from the mind of a hard-nosed business-man. It is, however, a self-evident and scientific fact. Every successful business comes from nothing. Every creative idea springs from nowhere. Before somebody had the idea, it did not exist.

In my own experiences, the ideas for companies and investments popped into my head quite out of nowhere. It is important to realize this fact because in most cases people are just too busy to notice. They could pop up while a mother is tearing her hair out getting the kids ready for school. The ideas never stood a chance, crushed by the anxiety of racing to meet the school bus. Perhaps they arise while watching television, but the images of a Wall Street crash will destroy them before the thinker even notices.

In my own cases of good ideas, they remained in my head, and became reality only because I had learned to have stronger control of my mentality. The world screamed through the television at me that it was a crazy time to start something new, and everyone I knew, other than my wife, didn't think I was capable of succeeding. Without knowing the techniques to control mentality, the ideas would have been crushed in moments.

The concept of nothing is difficult for us to compute mentally. As soon as we try to conceptualize it, we give it identity and form, and it ceases to be nothing. In essence, we destroy it by thinking about it. So let's not try too hard. The only thing to contemplate, and the only reason I make the distinction, is that because everything comes from nothing, then in nothing must be all of potential. The closer, therefore, we can get our minds to a state of nothing, the more potential for success we would have. We will come back to this in step two.

A thought is a thing that you created out of the nothing. Thoughts can be identified by modern imaging techniques as waves of electrical energy flowing in the brain. Having been created, thoughts have three fascinating properties:

1. **Thoughts are high energy.**

First, we must accept that all things have energy, which can be scientifically identified as a frequency of vibration at a quantum level, or a small footprint in the ether, or indeed, waves of electrical impulses.

Over the past three decades, *string theory* has increasingly captured the imagination of physicists. Hundreds of researchers around the world now hammer away at its equations every day. They consider it the greatest step forward in science since Albert Einstein and Max Planck introduced the key ideas of relativity and quantum mechanics about a century ago. It is what Einstein described as "like reading the mind of God."

String theory holds that everything in the universe is composed of tiny vibrating strings of energy. In this view, every particle in your body, every speck of light that lets you read these words, and every force of gravity that pushes you into your chair is just a variant of this one fundamental entity. The denser something is, the lower its vibration, and the smaller its footprint.

On our world, humans interpret a stone as being denser than a tree, and vibrating at a slower frequency. A tree is denser than a human. After nothingness, a thought is the least dense thing in our experience. Therefore, its first intriguing property is that it has the highest energy of anything we can conceptualize. It can kill or cure, invent a nuclear weapon or a romantic moment.

2. **Energy cannot be destroyed, so no thought can ever be deleted.**

The Law of Conservation of Energy is a law of physics that states the total amount of energy in an isolated system (such as a thought) remains constant over time. It cannot be destroyed, and it does not deplete if we simply forget we had it. Einstein's theory of relativity shows that mass is energy, and the two are interchangeable. Energy becomes mass and vice versa. A thought has no other role than to try to become its physical equivalent (mass). Therefore, because their energy remains conserved, the reality of your life experience today is the result of the thoughts you emitted in your life up to now, regardless of whether you remember having them. You may not accept that accountability right now, but I hope by the end of this book you will both understand and accept that your current experience is the result of prior thoughts and your reaction to them.

3. Thoughts are neutral.

The third, and somewhat disturbing, property of a thought is that it has no consciousness with which to assess the merits of itself. The thought itself does not think. It does not judge itself as good or bad. It simply exists as an isolated system. Therefore, all thoughts, whether we consider them good or bad ones to have, contain equal power to become reality.

Ah, there's the rub. Every thought eventually becomes its own experience, energy converted into matter, without considering if that is good or bad for us. This is why control of mentality is critical to your success. Whatever you are *against* becomes your experience, and you get extra helpings of what you did not want: more dead-end job, more stupid boss, and more boredom. Whatever you are *for*, more of that comes your way. The only solution is to have more *for* thoughts than *against* thoughts, and to make those *for* thoughts bigger. That is the simple lifestyle change required to control mentality.

Properties of Words

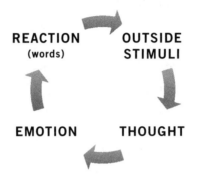

Lincoln scholar Douglas L. Wilson wrote: "To approach Lincoln's presidency from the aspect of his writing is to come to grips with the degree to which his pen, to alter the proverb, became his sword, arguably his most powerful presidential weapon." He noted that President Lincoln "responded to almost every important development during his presidency, and to many that were not so important, with some act of writing. Every word spoken, every line written was carefully mapped out."

Theodore C. Blegen wrote, in a study of Lincoln's writings: "He respected the power of words, and he wrote and spoke with clarity. He was able to put profound thoughts simply. He was sincere and earnest. He had both dignity and humor. He could rise to a lofty eloquence that has not been surpassed in the history of oratory. His language was pungent."

When not in control of our mentality, our immediate reaction to a thought is usually to issue words, whether texted, written, or verbalized. We may react in other ways such as kicking a wall, crying, or laughing, but most times the habitual reaction issues in words. When we are emotional, the tongue can react like a semi-automatic weapon in the hands of a poltergeist. It is an issue for us because all words immediately trigger images.

In 2011, researchers demonstrated, by implanting electrodes directly into a part of participants' brains, a striking method to reconstruct words, based on the brain waves of patients who were thinking of those words. The technique, reported in *PLoS Biology* in 2012, relies on gathering electrical signals directly from patients' brains. Based on signals from listening to patients, a computer model was used to reconstruct the sounds of words of which patients were thinking.

A research team at the University of California, Berkeley monitored the brain waves of fifteen patients who were undergoing surgery for epilepsy or tumors, while playing audio of a number of different speakers reciting words and sentences. With the help of a computer model, when patients were presented with words to think about, the team was able to calculate which word the participants had chosen. They were even able to reconstruct some of the words, turning the brain waves they saw back into sound on the basis of what the computer model suggested those waves meant.

For example, if I tell you to try not to think of an elephant wearing pajamas, an image of just that flashes in your mind. You can't read, hear, or say "elephant wearing pajamas" without imagining it. Our brains are wired to trigger images from words and words from images instantaneously.

A news bulletin just in says a highly placed person, close to the scene of the incident, and speaking on condition of anonymity, reported that the allegedly drunken elephant, wearing pink pajamas, tripped over a stone, crashed negligently into a tree, and rolled hopelessly out of control down a hill before plummeting into a raging sea.

Because of the use of emotive words, that image will stay in your mind even longer. The combination of words and emotive language has a powerful effect on our brains. (It is, however, a story with a happy ending because elephants are remarkable swimmers and have been known to swim across oceans. This elephant turned up safe and was found innocent of all charges.)

There are many books available about the power of words. The only property that concerns us in the *Three Simple Steps* is that words trigger images, images trigger thoughts, and thoughts become reality. We must consider words as magic bullets that carry the power to create or destroy. Cast like a spell from a voice, pen, or keyboard, they have the ability to make or break us. They also have the power to energize or diminish anyone at whom we fire them.

Being aware of the properties of thoughts and the power of emotion-laden words gives you the toolbox to control mentality and maintain individual thought.

Imagine this scenario: you are sitting down to watch your favorite television program when a 30-second commercial tells you about a quick loan that can take away those expensive monthly credit card payments. Although you have no interest in the offer and see it for the snake-oil solution it is, that outside stimuli immediately creates in your mind an image of the credit card bill you received a few days ago, the one you have hidden in a drawer in the hopes it will go away.

You immediately think about how much you hate being trapped in debt. The thought *debt* is launched with the emotion of being *against* it. Without you realizing it, you just increased your burden. That thought has no option but to become the material equivalent. Even though it was triggered by outside stimuli, it is still your thought, and the material equivalent comes back to you as the source of the thought. Something will happen in your environment to continue your sense of outrage at being in debt. A storm might rage that night and you wake next morning to find you have the only house on the street that lost some roof tiles. Because you have no cash, you also have no choice but to go further into credit card debt to fix the damage.

You curse out loud. "This sucks! I hate being in debt." The words shoot into the universe with only a little less power than thoughts. Those words trigger further images of you not being able to afford a vacation this year or the look of disappointment on your child's face when she can't have the brand of shoes she has been craving. The images happen so fast that you are barely aware of them.

The result will be that the experiences that show up in your life ensure you cannot afford to go on vacation, and your daughter is ashamed of her shoes. You might now feel like putting your foot through the television screen whenever that advertisement reruns, but it is a lot easier just to change how you react to your thoughts. The responsibility for them is yours. You own the thoughts and words. The difference between being in or out of the quicksand is merely taking responsibility for how you react to what you think. *Simple.*

Before I fully understood this, a friend and I worked in the same place. We had similar backgrounds, lifestyles, and challenges. She has watched me climb out of the quicksand and live an adventure that could be a book on its own. She, however, still works in the same job, one she now claims to hate. Her lifestyle has diminished in real terms over the years, and she is mired in debt. A doctor recently prescribed antidepressants for her.

Over many dinners, we have debated the importance of managing mentality. For some reason, she has never grasped this critical point about needing to direct one's own thoughts and words.

"How can it be?" she asks, "I don't want to be in debt. I hate debt. I'm fed up with always having to watch the pennies. When I don't want it, why do I keep getting it?"

I explain that the thought about not wanting debt manifests as a physical match of itself . . . the situation of not wanting debt. Something will happen in her life that will increase the hatred of debt. It is often an unexpected repair bill, but sometimes it's a "too good to refuse" offer for a piece of clothing, kitchen utensil, etc. Equally, it could be the tearful eyes of her son when he wants a new bike to be cool like his friends. She can't stand to see him upset, so she uses the credit card to buy what she cannot yet afford.

The more we think about not wanting something, the more we are against it and reinforce that situation in our lives. The answer is simple, but my friend refuses to change. If she managed the thoughts in her head, created images of things she really did want, and carefully controlled what she said in person or over social media, her life would improve.

A Tip to Help

Although simple to conceptualize, it is not an easy thing to do in practice because we are all creatures of habit. To help me to remember the power of my thoughts and words, I borrowed a trick from my favorite classic novel, *Far From the Madding Crowd* by Thomas Hardy. Set in a time when word of mouth was the most common way to communicate and lack of clarity could be life-threatening, Gabriel fails to impress the woman he secretly loves: "Well, Miss—excuse the words—I thought you would like them. But I can't match you, I know, in mapping out my mind upon my tongue."

Mapping your mind onto your tongue is a great way to visualize mentality control. When that credit card bill arrives, you should replace your angry thoughts with a smile. Take a pause, and a deep breath, and think about your reaction. Map it out on your tongue with the same care as if you were drawing directions for someone. Say to yourself something like "I am debt-free, and celebrated my last credit card payment with a glass of my favorite wine, purchased with cash."

Even though that is not your current experience, by thinking and speaking about what you really want, what you are *for*, rather than what you are *against*, you create the possibility of a better outcome. Better thoughts go out into the universe. The words you used have triggered even better images of a happy family sharing in your success, and the emotional feeling of a weight lifting off your shoulders. All those new thoughts and images have no choice but to become your reality. It might not happen overnight, but when consistently practiced, this small lifestyle change will have dramatic effects on your experiences.

Some might say this all sounds mysterious, but it is the basic physical law of conservation of energy. People generally accept it holds true in the laboratory or in nature. They do not, however, usually consider how it must hold true in their own lives. To get out of the quicksand, create better thoughts and words. That is all it takes. Until you habitually do this, it will prove hard to reinvent yourself and get that better life you want. Start with small steps in situations that we encounter many times a day.

Change a Little, Change a Lot, Every Day

Most of you can recall a time when you were feeling perfectly well, and then a colleague at work says, "Are you feeling okay? You look tired." Suddenly, a picture of you looking tired flashes in your mind, with gray skin and bags under your eyes. Perhaps a memory of when you were last sick cuts in. You recall you went to bed late last night, and although you had not felt tired until then, it makes sense that you should. Very quickly, those thoughts change into their material equivalent. I have lost count of the number of times I have overheard this sort of conversation, and then the recipient says something like "Now that you mention it, I do feel a bit weary."

- If you don't feel well or do feel tired, never tell anyone that. Instead, tell them "I could use more energy" or "once I am fit and healthy, I'll be fine." Every time you say something like "I'm feeling depressed" or "I feel down today," you are simply adding to your burden, albeit unintentionally. I had an appointment yesterday in which the person attending to me told me twelve times in twenty minutes how depressed she felt because of a personal crisis in her life. With every statement I could see the weight pressing down on her. A normally tall, straight, attractive woman, she looked stooped and weary. As much as I felt sympathy for her, I wanted to cut out her tongue to save her.

- Avoid use of limiting words such as "cannot" when referring to yourself. Instead, reach for a higher energy statement such as: "When I can . . ." Avoid using the words "perhaps," "hopefully," "one day," and "maybe" because when you use those words, what you are really saying is "I'd like to but I can't," and the universe hears your thoughts clearly.

- Eliminate destructive words such as "hate" from your vocabulary. For instance, replace "I hate it when that happens . . . " with "I prefer it when . . ." Again, we do not need to be perfect, and I mess up plenty of times. We just need to attempt a few small changes to make a big improvement in outcome. Before I wrote this section, I was with a friend who kept telling me how much he hates his job. He has been telling me that for almost fifteen years. All those words can do is trigger thoughts and images that return to him, so he gradually finds himself getting more of what he doesn't want.

- Begin and end every process of communication positively. Today, this is especially important when using electronic media. It is imperative that the last thing you type is a positive word leading to positive thoughts. So many people just sign off with an initial when a small positive word will work wonders. Try "Best," "Keep smiling," or "Cheers." Because you wrote it, you get the benefit. The recipient reads it, gets an image of a smiling friend, and now they get a positive jab too. Little changes, big outcomes.

- Begin and end your day positively. Before you go to sleep at night, thank yourself for a great day. When you wake up, the first words in your head should be something like: *I feel absolutely fantastic, and I know today is brilliantly successful for me.*

- When no one is within earshot, speak the words aloud. This may feel at first like the onset of insanity, but soon you'll be able to afford the best psychiatrists that money can hire.

- Whenever something irritates or depresses you during the day, take a deep breath, and silently pump yourself back up with an affirming statement. (Editors rightly admonish writers like me about overuse of adverbs and adjectives. Written sentences are better for their omission. On the trip to success, however, they are your best friends. They add emotion to the thought. Saying "I feel well" is acceptable for a novel. In life, saying "I feel absolutely, amazingly, vibrantly healthy!" takes you to a higher level of energy. It pumps you up faster. It is a really, really, really great thing to do.)

So far, we have analyzed the equation in reverse order, and some readers might consider the information on controlling thoughts and words as only a little different than extolling the virtues of positive thinking or the power of positive words. This is, however, something that you can begin right now and change your life. It requires no monetary investment, no time, and only a little effort. From this moment on, before you speak, take a little breath, smile, pause . . . and then map out your better thoughts in stronger words onto your tongue. Just try it for a day and see how differently things work out for you.

In my experience, people often come to grips with this aspect easily, but very quickly something negative happens at work or home or they take notice of something emotionally draining that is on television, and all the good work is undone in a flash. Controlling our thoughts and words is part of the essential process, but it becomes much more powerful if we can manage the stimuli that trigger them as well.

CONTROLLING SENSORY INPUT

A thousand things can cause you to have a thought and react with a word, but we only need to make small changes in our lifestyles to achieve great things. In this step, we are concerned with only two main sources of stimuli.

One of the main influences in our immediate environment is the chronic complainer. Nothing unites people more closely than a common dislike, which means we often find ourselves bonded to people who are *against* something or someone. That becomes a downward-spiraling energy wave, leading back to quicksand.

The other main influence is the media, in all its forms. Some of it may be harmless entertainment, but whether selling a product or an ideology, it is clear that political, religious, and business institutions understand how to sculpt common thinking. The people who work in those institutions may not know they can control their own destiny, but they are fully aware of their ability to make groups of people behave in a certain way. They go to great effort and expense to invade your environment and march unopposed against your mentality.

Why should we care about these influences? It is because thoughts must become matter that returns to the owner of the thought. So, if you see something in the media or hear something from a person nearby, that causes you to trigger a negative thought-image, and the material realization of that comes into your life, not the thing or person that caused your thought.

The problem is compounded by the simple fact that, in order to influence us, people or media must hold our attention long enough to create a reaction. Fear paralyzes. It works better than any other emotion to keep us entranced long enough for whatever message they have. Media and people tend to hold us fixated by making us feel anxious, perhaps with gossip, a rumor, or a dramatic headline.

The effects of fear are important to understand if you want to get out of the quicksand. As soon as you feel fear, the amygdala (a small, almond-shaped organ in the center of your brain) sends signals to your autonomic nervous system, producing a wide range of effects. Your heart rate increases, your blood pressure goes up, your breathing gets quicker, and stress hormones such as adrenaline and cortisol are released.

Robert Sapolsky, a professor of neuroendocrinology at Stanford University, has focused his research on issues of stress and neural degeneration. He has won many honors for his papers that show links between long-term stressful life experiences, long-term exposure to hormones such as cortisol, produced during stress, and shrinking of the hippocampus area of the brain.

The hippocampus is a mass of neurons, each with multiple branch-like extensions (dendrites and axons) that make connections (synapses) with other neurons all across the brain. The hippocampus is also one of the few regions of the brain known to be able to produce new neurons, a process called neurogenesis.

Professor Sapolsky has shown that enduring a high stressor,

like watching fearful news or listening to someone spread a stressful rumor at work, for more than thirty minutes, negatively impacts the hippocampus in various ways. To begin, sustained exposure to higher than normal levels of cortisol results in the pruning back of the number of branches and synaptic connections of hippocampal neurons. By a variety of mechanisms, these conditions also increase the rate of cell death in this region of the brain.

As if this wasn't bad enough, recent research is demonstrating that sustained increases in glucocorticoid levels also have negative effects, impairing the hippocampus's ability to create new neurons. Over a period of time, all of this results in the shrinking in size of the hippocampus with associated declines in cognitive function, including the ability to retain new information and adapt to new situations, *which is exactly what you don't want when you are attempting to reinvent your life.*

Fortunately, according to Sapolsky, the negative effects of excessive stress can not only be stopped but reversed "once the source, psychological or physical, is removed or sufficiently reduced." Simple! Change a little, change a lot.

Chronic Complainers

Think about the day you have had so far. How many times did someone complain about something to you directly or within your hearing? It may have been a trivial matter like the weather or something significant they saw in the newspaper such as the state of the economy. How often did you automatically join in? Did you start a chat by having a little moan about something? Think about all of your Twitter posts, texts, and emails and which of them were critical of a thing or person.

Although the criticisms may be slight, they accumulate in the course of a day into an avalanche of negativity that raises anxiety.

It is scary when you stop to think about it and realize how many of the words being mapped out are negative. Whether verbal, written, or electronic, they have the same impact.

Many people revel in gossip and rumor mongering. It bonds them quickly and is the easiest way to make allies. Because it's so contagious, we can slip into the habit innocently. It holds groups together like glue, and you cannot reinvent yourself as part of a group. The aim is for you to become an individual again.

Gossip is toxic to our mentality. Every time we allow a complaint into our brains, it triggers a negative thought that has no choice but to return more of what is being complained about to us. If someone bemoans the economy, and you think "I agree with that," then events will transpire in your life that give you even more reason to moan about it . . . even though you did not initiate the topic and were thinking of something completely different earlier.

Another good exercise is to sit with friends or family and listen to their comments as you all watch a soap opera or reality television show. Almost everything is negative because the shows are designed and written to trigger that reaction. I did this with two relatives once and counted more than a hundred negative statements from them in less than a half hour.

Every criticism is a form of being *against.* As painful as it is to consider, whatever someone is against comes back like a boomerang to the thrower, which increases exposure to the harmful effects of stress even more. Of course, if you say something positive, that shows up in your life also, but the challenge is that nothing unites people more than a common dislike. Positive people are a rarity and, unfortunately, most successful people must walk a solo path.

If you reached the end of your days, then added up the beneficial vs. harmful thoughts and came out 51 percent to 49 percent in favor of beneficial, you would have lived a grand adventure. Most people, however, would be more than 80 percent negative, and their lives would be a reflection of that. Our aim with this step is just to shift the balance more toward neutral. If you doubt it, spend a day and a night keeping score. Make a note of every positive comment you hear and every negative one. It will shock you.

This is a national and cultural disease in the Western world. We are a society of complainers. I am not complaining about it. I am just stating a fact. I find complainers a source of amusement, and usually tease them mercilessly by reacting completely differently to the way they expect. In a recent comment on this subject in the *San Francisco Chronicle*, I read:

> Our complaining begins to curdle, to turn back on itself, poison the heart, turns us nasty and low. It shifts from merely being a national mood or general temperament into a way of being; a wiring, deep, and harmful, and permanent.

That writer was onto something, because whatever we allow into our minds begins to rewire our neural networks. A recent study, published in *Behavioural Brain Research*, September 2011, conducted by researchers from the Department of Biological and Clinical Psychology at Friedrich Schiller University in Germany, measured the neural effect of negative and positive words versus neutral words. This functional MRI study showed positive vs. negative words led to increased activation in the ventral medial prefrontal cortex, which is associated with risk, fear, and decision-making processes, while negative vs. positive words induced increased activation of the insula, which is thought to impact perception, motor control, self-awareness, cognitive functioning, and interpersonal experience.

In business, I am always looking for the "so what" aspect to everything. *Don't give me facts and features—tell me the benefit* is the mantra of any successful sales consultation. With these sort of studies, I am often left with a "so what" feeling, like a great film without a conclusion. What does it really mean?

In his book on neuroplasticity, *The Brain That Changes Itself: Stories of Personal Triumph from the Frontiers of Brain Science,* Norman Doidge, M.D., states plainly that the brain has the capacity to rewire itself and/or form new neural pathways—if we do the work. Just like exercise, the work requires repetition and activity to reinforce new learning.

So complaining repetitively can become a wired thing in your brain, deep and harmful. We can all think of someone who seems incapable of speaking without complaining. The good news is that by controlling mentality, the damage does not have to be permanent. Even better news is that in the second part of this book, we will spend time on rewiring our neurons to the way we *want* them to be and completely reversing the damage already done.

The tendency for Americans to complain comes partly from a chronic sense of disappointment. Americans are naturally outgoing and optimistic. Expectations are generally high. If you have been to the United Kingdom, you'll understand the contrast with British pessimism.

Americans are the only people who are genuinely surprised and disappointed when politicians do not keep their promises. In other countries, people are just relieved if their leaders get through their terms of office without being mired in a sadomasochistic sex scandal. Americans expect the economy always to be growing, house prices to rise continuously, and everyone to be better off in the future than they are now. Because life is a series of peaks and valleys, it sets up a rollercoaster of feeling excited and let down. It is important to recognize this because the trip to success is more undulating than linear.

As an Englishman who moved to America, however, I have a different perspective and find little to complain about. I have lived in five states, each one a different cultural experience. If I don't like the weather, I can simply move to a place with a better climate instead of complaining all the time about the one I inhabit. No one dictates where I have to reside. I need no visa to move.

Education is available to all. Everyone can get a degree, even if it is in hamburger technology. Those with degrees in hamburger technology become professional servers. This is the only nation that has waiters who smile when they serve food. Go to England or France and then complain to the waiter that your food is a little cold and see what happens. Go to Spain and tell the maître d' that you are tired of waiting for service. You'll be seated at your table a year from now. Americans have service down to a fine art.

Restaurants deliver quality food to your front door at night and on a Sunday! Stores are open when people need them, like after office hours. Grocery stores burst with a mind-boggling variety of foods. The checkout people are friendly, and someone packs your groceries into bags for you. On top of that, sales tax is less than 20 percent, which is the rate in more than thirty-six countries around the globe!

When I left England, not only did I have to pay 18 percent sales tax on everything, but my income tax was at a rate of 48 percent with 8 percent compulsory national insurance. For every £100 I earned, I could only purchase £26 worth of groceries with the disposable income I had left. Now, that is reason to complain. In America, however, I live in a state with no income tax and a sales tax under 9 percent, but everyone I know complains about their taxes.

When I go to a public place in America, no one is allowed to attempt to kill me with cigarette smoke. I can walk on the sidewalk without being ankle deep in litter, or having to dodge presents left by dogs. Cursing is practically a capital offence, and nudity is not allowed at the beach. (Okay, so not everything in America is better.)

Gasoline is a fraction of what it costs in European countries, and Americans can have a car for each foot. I can drive almost anywhere. I can effectively live my whole life in a car, never starve, and end it at a drive-through funeral parlor.

Best of all, an immigrant like me, one with no identifiable skill, can come up with an idea to start a business. I can succeed simply because I have control of my mentality. No one cares from which class of society I came. No one minds if I had the right schooling or family connections, which are so vital in other countries. In America, absolutely anyone can do and be anything they choose. What is there to complain about?

What happened to the American pioneering spirit, the can-do attitude? Almost everyone reading this book will have ancestors who came from somewhere else, clothed in little more than a will to succeed. Where did that spirit go that is so rarely seen in America today? Everyone seems afraid to get out of the quicksand these days.

I came to America believing in the possibility of the American dream. It was a while before I bought a television or newspaper, so I never heard all the people complaining about the dream being dead. If you ask me, the American dream is alive and well. You do, however, have to get out of the quicksand to find it and live it.

Here is a simple task that will open your eyes. Tomorrow, make a conscious effort not to join in all the complaining or to start a complaint yourself. When you hear someone complain, tune out. Turn the radio station to a positive channel. Avoid the coffee station at work, and go get some fresh air at lunchtime. When anyone around you tries to bait you with a chronic complaint, smile and excuse yourself. When someone on the phone is complaining of a health or other problem, make a quick excuse and put down the receiver. Don't get sucked into a negative discussion, just for this single day. At the end of the day, compare how much more energy you have that day to the day before. Check your mood in the evening. Don't you feel happier and lighter? Don't you feel like you really could reinvent yourself today?

Tips for Dealing with Complainers

1. Become self-aware.

The first step toward recovery is to recognize when you are about to complain. Every time you feel a complaint coming on, no matter how trivial, stop yourself. You cannot delete a thought, but you can have a better thought. When you catch yourself in the middle of a complaint, stop, and then reach for a better thought. My wife used to go window-shopping with a friend. Looking at something she desired, her friend would always comment, "Oh, that's nice, but I could never afford it. It is crazy to spend that much on a piece of clothing. Look, that's a whole month's wages. Insane!"

Like me, my wife knows to control her state of mind. She would pause before commenting, "That will look wonderful with my black trousers, when I can afford to buy it." If you were to visit both homes and inspect the closets, you would see the outcome of this small change in mapping thoughts out on her tongue. My wife has beautiful clothes. Her friend still shops at the thrift store and bemoans the fact that she cannot buy nice things. There is nothing wrong with that, but it does not have to be her experience.

2. Redirect the conversation.

One of the hardest places to be aware of your mentality is during spontaneous conversation. First, you must catch yourself in the act of negativity and stop the words of complaint before they come out. Then consciously replace what the *old you* would have said. Imagine you have just walked into the office:

COLLEAGUE: Hey, man, how's it going?
OLD YOU: Not bad. You?
COLLEAGUE: Tired. Weekend is not long enough.
OLD YOU: I hear you. Sick of this weather. I can't remember the last time we saw the sun. I spent all last night shoveling the drive. My back's killing me.
COLLEAGUE: You're getting old, man. What can you do? You going to the staff meeting later?
OLD YOU: Nah, got too much to catch up on. Got to get Jim those market reports or he'll be on my back all day.
COLLEAGUE: He's a pain in the ass.
OLD YOU: You got that right.

The energy created by this early morning exchange is low. Misery loves company, and the two of you feel like comrades, united by a common dislike of the weather and Jim. Read it again and you will count twelve complaints in that one small exchange. We have dozens of conversations like this every day. Knowing the importance of mentality, the *new you* would take control of the situation this way:

COLLEAGUE: Hey, man, how's it going?
NEW YOU (pauses, maps out words carefully): Fantastic, thanks. You?
COLLEAGUE: Tired. Weekend is not long enough.
NEW YOU: I could always use more energy as well. I hope we'll see some sun this week. That'll give us a boost.

COLLEAGUE: You bet. You going to the staff meeting later?

NEW YOU: I'd like to. It will be good to catch up with everyone after the weekend. But I must get some reports to Jim beforehand.

COLLEAGUE: He's a pain in the ass.

NEW YOU (pauses, maps out words carefully): I'm sure he needs them. I should have done them last night, but I started shoveling snow off the drive and ended up building a snowman with the kids. What a blast! They loved it. Well, better get started. Have a great morning, and see you later at the meeting.

The difference in energy created for you is remarkable. The language is positive, the images and thoughts creative. You will not feel as bonded to your colleague, and don't be surprised if he tries to bring your energy down later. Right now, he thinks aliens have taken over your body. You will, however, feel your day is off to a better start. If you consciously try to control a dozen conversations a day, reaching for positive words and thoughts as often as you can, you will create a storehouse of powerful energy.

3. Be kind to yourself.

We are not trying to be perfect. We all trip up and fall back to the habit of complaining. Whenever I play or watch my favorite sport, which is soccer, I seem to leave everything I know about *Three Simple Steps* behind. To err is human. It happens. When it happens, smile and start afresh. Treat it like a game.

4. Smother a negative thought with a positive image.

If I am leaving the house and the thought comes to mind that the weather sucks, I immediately input a different image. A picture of a lazy summer day spent lying beside a babbling stream flashes in my mind. Imagination is our savior. Replace every negative thought with a positive image. It takes only a moment.

5. Don't try to convert anyone.

Keep in mind that those around you feel comfortable in the company of a fellow complainer. If you try to stop them, you will likely succeed only in alienating yourself. In effect, you'll give those people more to complain about because they will target you. When trapped in the midst of complainers at a business meeting or a social engagement, simply choose silence. Let their words float by while you think of something more pleasant like a lovely day at the beach, the feel of your favorite pet's coat, or the soft kiss of a loved one. Eventually, people will stop trying to draw you in because you don't react the way they expect and need you to react. Like-minded people attract each other, and opposites repel. Before long, your common circle of associates will be refreshingly different.

6. Distance yourself when possible.

When people around you start criticizing someone or something and you can escape, excuse yourself and take a break somewhere quiet. If possible, go outside for fresh air. Think of something pleasant before returning. Remember, your life is at stake. You have to take this seriously. Don't let the negative influences of others pull you back into the quicksand. Often, I have stood up from a meeting table and turned to look out through a window while the complainers continue to vent their feelings behind me. It is a bit like breaking a séance circle, and the complaining soon stops. When it does, I sit back down.

7. **Wear an invisible "mentality shield."**

Imagine an invisible shield like a glass cloak descends from the sky and lightly covers your whole body. You can see perfectly well through it, and only you know it is there. It is made of the highest positive energy. Nothing anyone says can penetrate it. Negative emotions simply bounce off. You can imagine their words hitting it and exploding into meaningless letters. Their complaints disintegrate into nothing. No one in that room can get thoughts or images through to impact your state of mind.

This technique is used by many of the world's top athletes to protect themselves from the negative energy of a hostile crowd. I find it particularly useful in business settings. I never enter a meeting room without my shield in place. I also use it frequently around certain friends and family members who can be the source of most of the chronic complaints in my life.

8. **Create a private retreat.**

Mentally retreat to a private, special place in your imagination. For me, this is a ribbon of soft, white sand about one hundred yards across, arcing through a turquoise lagoon. While appearing interested in whatever sights and sounds are before me, I can walk my two miles of sand. I find this technique useful if stuck in the company of complainers at a dinner or while commuting and traveling. It especially helps when something in my travel schedule goes awry. If a plane is delayed on the runway, for instance, I retreat to my island while everyone around me gets more and more heated and negative.

What is your private retreat? It could be a sailboat or a warm cabin on a mountain summit—whatever makes you feel relaxed, positive, and at peace with yourself and the world around you. The more often you do this, the more detailed your private retreat becomes in your memory. By distracting your mind this way, you keep the door firmly shut to the negativity around you. The best aspect of this trick is that one day your retreat turns up in your physical reality. I mentally walked that ribbon of sand a hundred times before I got to do it for real. This is the joy of control of mentality. When one becomes so adept at it, even idle daydreams get to be experienced.

9. Transfer responsibility.

Finally, on the occasions you find yourself pressed back against a wall while someone rants and raves about all the injustices in their life, throw the responsibility back at them with, "So what do *you* intend to do about it?" In most cases, the complainers don't actually want a solution. They don't even want sympathy. They just want to react by venting anger. Throwing that question to them will stop them in their tracks.

Media

In *The Shipping News*, Lasse Hallstrom's adaptation of E. Annie Proulx's best seller, there is a scene in which the local newspaper editor confronts reporter Quoyle about his inability to find a storyline. Billy takes Quoyle to the edge of a cliff:

BILLY (EDITOR) [Points at dark clouds on the horizon]:
It's finding the center of your story, the beating heart of
it, that's what makes a reporter. You have to start by making up some headlines. You know: short, punchy, dramatic headlines. Now, have a look, what do you see?

BILLY: Tell me the headline.

QUOYLE: Horizon Fills with Dark Clouds?

BILLY: Imminent Storm Threatens Village.

QUOYLE: But what if no storm comes?

BILLY: Village Spared from Deadly Storm.

Almost all television news and newspapers exist to sell advertising space. If they fail to do that, the news media fail to exist.
To get good prices for the space, they need to guarantee an audience to their advertisers. To do that, they must grab our attention with a dramatic headline or image that draws us in and
then hold our attention long enough to get to an advertisement. Fear is generally their weapon of choice. Who can resist
watching a live car chase, a battle scene from a war zone, or the
threat of a tornado in the area? At this point, you might think
it's all harmless, but any sensational headline or news story has
the potential to induce fear into our systems.

The challenge we face with regard to the news media is that
the brain does not distinguish between that which is real and
that which is imagined. Watching a scene of carnage in a war
zone causes some of the same detrimental stress effects as actually being there ourselves. The fear response we have in
front of the television is the same we would have in the real
situation. Of course, it is diluted somewhat by the safety net of
our home, but people addicted to the news are subjecting
themselves to chronic stress every time they tune in. Day after
day, they take their dose of news and induce a cascade of de-
struction in their neurons.

To make matters worse, everything you see and hear in the media triggers images in your brain. If you watch a news report about a crime, the pictures in your brain are a reaction to the horror you are observing. Your eyes take in a stranger on the street being mugged, which at first might seem inconsequential. The emotion you feel, however, is not because you recognize the stranger but because you know how you would feel if that happened to you or someone you know. Many times, I hear people say "I don't know how I'd cope if that happened to me." The moment they say it, they imagine it, and those thoughts remain out in the universe with the potential to create exactly what they don't want. Every time you watch something fearful on television, you also place your life at risk because your thoughts have the propensity to convert to matter and come right back at you.

You should understand I am not antimedia—far from it. Media are simply vehicles for transmitting messages and can be valuable assets in our quest for knowledge and success. I enjoy a comedy, an educational documentary, or a film as much as anyone, and I watch a lot of sports. The key is in being selective in what media messages you allow into your brain, and then how you choose to react to them.

For instance, if you are in debt, then you should avoid those advertisements that offer debt solutions because of the effect on your thought generation as we discussed earlier. If, however, you desire to own a top-end Mercedes-Benz, then not only is it acceptable to watch those advertisements, you should record them and play them over and over until, instead of the actor in the driver's seat, you start to see yourself. You should call the toll-free number to request a brochure and more information. Then read the car reviews in the newspaper. Find your local dealer and go for a test drive. You should watch any show or film in which the car manufacturer has paid to have their vehicle used by the actors. The point is that we must be selective in what we allow into our minds, manage what we think about them, and control our reactions. We avoid what we are *against* and seek out what we are *for.*

Media marketing attempts to influence our behavior in remarkably simple ways. An unguarded state of mind can be shown an advertisement of a sexy girl, who appears attracted to a man smoking a particular brand of cigarette. As he watches, the viewer knows it is a carcinogenic poison. He knows his nicotine-stained hands, poised to hit the channel-change button before a girl in a bikini showed up, would turn off any female who looked like the one on the screen. His breath would send her to the nearest bathroom. His reaction, however, is to reach for a cigarette because he subconsciously fears being undesirable.

In my father's case, his reaction to this type of advertisement was to send me out to the store to buy some more cigarettes. When I was six, in the days when there was no age limit required for their purchase, he would send me to the corner store for an extra pack of his favorite filter-tipped brand. I once forgot what I had been sent for and brought home half a dozen eggs, a ball of wool, and some oranges. Audrey appreciated the wool, but a man deprived of his nicotine fix can launch eggs and oranges like missiles.

Media can also be vehicles for propaganda. Anyone with an idea that they want to share with others becomes a propagandist. The father of propaganda, long before the days of television, was Joseph Goebbels. In a famous 1928 speech on the means and power of propaganda, he stated:

> Propaganda stands between the idea and the worldview, between the worldview and the state, between the individual and the party, between the party and the nation. At the moment at which I recognize something as important and begin speaking about it in the streetcar, I begin making propaganda. At the

same moment, I begin looking for other people to join me. Propaganda stands between the one and the many, between the idea and the worldview. Propaganda is nothing other than the forerunner to organization. Once it has done this, it is the forerunner to state control. It is always a means to an end.

Propaganda in any format can erode the individual mindset, and we have to be aware of its influence on us. Are the opinions you have on various matters your own or have they been comfortably fused into your mind by propaganda?

I often have this discussion with a relative who has strong opinions about the members of the Royal Family in England. Her opinions have changed over time, depending on the images shown in newspapers and on television. I have met many of the Royal Family personally and formed my own opinion of them from those interactions. My impressions differ markedly from anything you would read in a tabloid newspaper or that my relative repeats thereafter as her own opinions.

When I remind my relative that she has never met these people, she will vehemently defend herself and her right to her own opinion. She admonishes me, even though in reality, her only source of information is what she has seen or heard through various media, often reinforced by her friends who share the same opinions.

In reality, since 1997, there has been a concerted public relations campaign run by a prominent global advertising agency, and costing millions, to repair the image of the Royal Family. The goal of the campaign was to "reposition the family into a unifying force."

In the same way as someone from Joseph Goebbel's time would distribute pamphlets to a crowd, the religious, political, and business institutions in our high-tech world use all the vehicles of modern media from television to social networks. The aim is to form a state of mind, bring like-minded people to-gether, and create a specific reaction. That might be to cause you to send a donation, vote a certain way, or buy a product. It could also be to encourage you to buy a house you can't afford or invest unwisely in daily stock trading with the money you could have used to start a business of your own.

In the mid-1980s, prior to the innovation of satellite televi-sion, I lived in the United Kingdom, where I was quite satisfied with three television channels. After heated debate, the govern-ment allowed a fourth network to start broadcasting. They needed innovative programs to draw audiences and picked up American football. A one-hour highlight show ran on Monday nights and, for the first time, Brits started to get into the game.

The program quickly got the highest ratings in the lineup. At the end of the season, the producers pulled a coup with the first live showing of a Super Bowl. Some friends and I got into the excitement and threw a party as Chicago played New England.

Our first mistake was miscalculating the time difference. The game kicked off at close to midnight, by which time most of us were highly inebriated. The second mistake was that no one re-alized there would be so many commercial breaks. A one-hour game took three hours to play. We had been used to the con-densed highlights show and did not expect the game to be so fragmented. Brought up on soccer and rugby, in which the games flow without commercial breaks or time-outs, by the end of the first quarter, no one remained conscious.

When I moved to America, I wanted to follow the sport. I could not, however, get beyond the number of commercial in-terruptions that seemed, to me at least, to be thinly disguised military propaganda. I was not judging it. I didn't have an opin-ion on the merits of US foreign policy, but I know propaganda when I see it, regardless of who produces it, and I don't allow it into my brain. I found it hard to tune out the jingoism and enjoy the sport. Hitting the mute button is not sufficient to protect my neurons from all that shock and awe.

Whether it is an army recruitment advertisement or a military commander involved in the coin toss, all those images can be dangerous to your state of mind. Most people, however, consider them harmless and think of themselves as being immune to the impact because they are seemingly passive background images. If your mentality is unguarded, they are anything but passive.

Nothing demonstrates the power of media marketing or the extremes of habitual reaction like that of a soldier going off to war. A poorly educated farm laborer, who knows nothing more than the art of tending dairy cattle, watches the threat of terrorism every night on the television news, absorbs the glorification of war in a stream of macho army recruitment commercials during his Sunday football television ritual, and drinks in his favorite reality television show being beamed live from the deck of an aircraft carrier. His reaction is to leave his farm, don a uniform, and travel to a place he could never have found in an atlas. Acting on orders, he shoots an "insurgent" because he believes his freedom on the plains of Ohio is threatened.

The insurgent was also a happy, world-unwise farm worker, tending goats in his own country. His unguarded state of mentality was convinced by different propaganda that was shouted from a shrine to react to a perceived threat. He left the field that his ancestors had farmed for centuries, strapped an explosive vest to his chest, and went to greet the "infidel" who just showed up.

As fellow farmers, with individual mindsets and opinions, the two should have had a lot in common. The possibility exists that, under different circumstances and with controlled mentalities, they could become friends, and share their farming stories.

More than ninety million people tuned into the 2012 Super Bowl half-time show to see a bunch of commercials. Forty-four percent of all female and thirty-one percent of all male viewers of the Super Bowl claimed to tune in just to watch the commercials. Most of them probably considered it harmless entertainment and thought they would be immune to its impact. If it were so harmless then why would advertisers be willing to spend $3.5 million for a 30-second commercial? Throughout the game, more than 100 commercials aired. In one advertisement, I counted the word *debt* mentioned ten times. If that advertisement was played five times during the game, it pressed four-and-a-half billion footprints of debt-thought into the ether, all of which, by the law of nature, must return back into the lives of those who generated them.

In an average year, a five-year-old sees forty thousand media advertisements. How does that impact a child's unguarded state of mind? Over a lifetime, how has that impacted adult mentality and eroded individual thought? Statistics show that advertising expenditures for debt reduction programs and weight loss products have grown exponentially in the last few years. At the same time, personal debt is at unprecedented levels and obesity is a national issue. But which came first?

Metaphors in several popular self-help books compare the mind to a fertile garden. The owner diligently uproots the occasional weed of negativity to replace it with a flower of positivity. New Age xylophones chime in the distance, hummingbirds flutter overhead, and readers everywhere reach for the stomach medicine.

In reality, we live in a complex, noisy world where negativity is all around. Controlling one's state of mind is more than keeping up with the weeding. It is like defending ourselves against the venomous plants of John Wyndham's 1951 novel, *The Day of the Triffids.*

When I was a child, those monsters terrified me. Whenever I think of negative media, that is what I imagine. For the uninitiated, triffids were tall plants with a deadly, whip-like, poisonous sting that enabled them to paralyze their victims and feed on their rotting carcasses. Advertising agencies must love that image. The marketing manager's sensational, 3-second headlines grab our attention, and hold us immobile while whatever message, subliminal or otherwise, is inserted into our neurons.

Everywhere you go, they lie in wait. Along the freeway, triffids crawl over advertisement boards to tell you how overweight you look today, how unattractive your bald patch, acne, or wrinkles appear, and how much better you would feel if you took out another high interest credit card for the joy of the reward points and to pay for the cosmetic makeover that you desperately need.

In the airport, they slither from television screens with messages of fear and doom. Behind newspaper stands, they spew out gloom about an economy on the brink of collapse while the rich, fat bankers escape. "Who in their right mind would go against the crowd and want to reinvent themselves in such a climate? What mad individual would think of starting a company now?" are the opinions you hear just after another great idea for a company of your own popped into your head.

In fact, as previously mentioned, sixteen of the thirty companies that make up the Dow Jones Industrial Average were started during a recession. These include Procter & Gamble, Disney, Alcoa, McDonald's, and Johnson & Johnson. After every recession, there is an upsurge in the pioneering spirit that is unique to America. I started my first company right in the middle of the 2001–2003 recession. There is no such thing as a bad time to start over.

When discussing the influences of media messaging with any group, I always get the same reaction. Everyone in the room knows what I am talking about. No one disagrees with me. Then, each person looks accusingly at everyone else. I can tell that each person thinks he or she is the only one immune to the influence. That is how we react to any form of propaganda. We recognize that our enemies use propaganda against us, so we filter that out. We don't expect propaganda to be coming at us from within our society, so we innocently let it in, and it can impact how we react as the next story shows:

Liverpool is a city of fewer than a million residents, but it boasts the eighth richest sports club in the world: their main soccer team. Soccer is like an elixir that runs through the veins of everyone.

A few years ago, a tabloid newspaper printed front-page photographs of a famous soccer player as he left an alleged brothel.

The day after the tabloid photographs, a local radio station ran a report in which two witnesses recounted having watched the soccer player and his fiancée arguing in a city center park. They told how the soccer player pleaded his innocence, but with front-page photograph in her hand, the girlfriend screamed accusations. In a gesture of anger, they said, she wrenched off her engagement ring and threw it into the flowerbeds.

That afternoon, the same radio station transmitted a live report from the park, where police had been called to quell a riot. After hearing the first bulletin, a crowd of enterprising locals, wielding spades, forks, and metal detectors, descended on the area. The flowerbeds were churned into a mud bath. Turf war broke out as, like pioneers in the Gold Rush, people staked claims to different patches of garden. A dozen victims were rushed to the hospital with head injuries from spade duels. One opportunistic youth relocated a bulldozer from a building site. He was arrested not just for the theft but for charging the others by the hour for his digging services.

Later, it emerged that the first bulletin had been severely edited. The reporter's full story included the news that once the soccer player had left, the girlfriend returned to the park to retrieve her ring. The editor thought it an unnecessarily long piece of journalism, and cut the story off at the point the ring was discarded. The radio station made a formal apology, but more than sixty budding entrepreneurs spent the night in jail.

No one is immune. I am suggesting that you be aware of the potential negative impact on your mentality of not controlling sensory input. Be selective. Remember, small changes in behavior produce big changes in outcome.

Dealing with Media—Steps to Take

1. **Selectively turn off the television and radio news.**

    Because we want to reduce the release of stress chemicals on our neurons, and almost all news stories are about something frightening and negative, avoid watching or listening as much as you can. You will be surprised to find that you still remain informed because it is impossible to escape completely. That is okay. What you are trying to avoid are the negative emotions that accompany the sensational headlines; if you find that you can't switch off the channel, then at least mute the volume. After a few months, you will find this is liberating. Some people describe it as a weight being lifted from their shoulders. That is because they no longer have all that fear and anxiety increasing their stress levels, and destroying their neurons.

2. **Avoid advertisements that trigger negative images in your mind.**

    Different things will be a source of fear for different people, so you have to be selective. For instance, if I see an advertisement today for a credit card, it does not bother me because I am no longer worried about debt. Twenty years ago, however, my internal stress reaction would have been very different when the emotions of debt were being spewed from the television. I had to learn to tune those out of my life.

Think about how you respond internally to certain types of commercials, and how that might impact your neurons. At the very least, mute the television and look away when any of those advertisements come on. Your life is at stake, so why risk it? For your favorite programs, use the DVR, and fast-forward through the commercials that might affect you.

They are not all bad, of course, and many are pure entertainment. I always get a laugh out of the quack ones that sell miracle metal bracelets without ever making a medical claim. "I used to have arthritis and now would never be without my bracelet" or the countertop ovens that have such poor insulation "you can even boil up some vegetables just by placing a pan on the top." The point again is to be selective; small changes in habit result in vast improvements in outcome.

My favorites are the cigarette advertisements from the first half of the twentieth century. When advertising was unregulated, those companies could make any claim they wanted. "Seven out of ten doctors recommend our brand of cigarettes" is a classic. The best I ever saw was a magazine page that showed a cartoon drawing of a double-decker bus hurtling toward a naïve couple who smiled at us from the page, unaware that in just a few seconds they were to be crushed. The tagline was *Go on . . . have a smoke!* The inference was that we could get run over by a bus at any moment, so why not just enjoy oneself. Apart from the absurdity of it, what made me smile the most was that the advertisement did not favor any particular brand of tobacco. Smoke anything, it screamed . . . a chair leg, the bus exhaust . . . just smoke something before you die!

3. Seek independent reporting.

To succeed, all propaganda has to be popular, and has to accommodate itself to the comprehension of the least intelligent of those whom it seeks to reach.

ADOLPH HITLER

We all know that people's mentalities can be easily manipulated because we can see it in everyone else. The danger is we never see this same vulnerability in ourselves. If the knowledge that all network news and newspapers are merely tools of someone's propaganda is news to you, start to read alternative versions of events as presented by independent journalists. Here are the two I follow most closely and recommend for their politically neutral and objective investigative journalism:

■ *John Pilger (johnpilger.com):* Pilger has won an Emmy and a BAFTA for his documentaries, which have also won numerous awards in the United States and Europe. His articles appear worldwide in newspapers such as the *Guardian*, the *Independent*, the *New York Times*, the *Los Angeles Times*, the *Mail & Guardian* (South Africa), *Aftonbladet* (Sweden), and *Il Manifesto* (Italy). He writes a regular column for the *New Statesman*, published in London. In 2001, he curated a major exhibition at the London Barbican, *Reporting the World: John Pilger's Eyewitness Photographers*, a tribute to the great black-and-white photographers with whom he has worked. In 2003, he was awarded the prestigious Sophie Prize for "30 years of exposing injustice and promoting human rights." In 2009, he was awarded the Sydney Peace Prize. His latest film is *The War You Don't See* (2010).

- *Greg Palast (gregpalast.com):* He is the author of the *New York Times* and international best sellers, *The Best Democracy Money Can Buy* and *Armed Madhouse*. Palast is Patron of the Trinity College Philosophical Society, an honor previously held by Jonathan Swift and Oscar Wilde. Palast directed documentaries covering the US government's largest racketeering case in history and the investigation of the *Exxon Valdez* disaster. He is the recipient of the George Orwell Courage in Journalism Prize for his television documentary, *Bush Family Fortunes.*

4. Reach for a better image.

Any time you catch yourself reading a sensational headline, make a point of retreating to the private mental place you have created. Force yourself to smile and contemplate that pleasant image or memory. It is essential to counter the energy drain that just occurred when you let something fearful into your mind.

5. Keep your eyes facing front at the checkout counter.

Do not pick up that gossip magazine at the grocery store checkout counter. Don't read the cover headlines. Hard, isn't it? Those gossip triffids screech the loudest, and they have you corralled into a small space with no escape. Those publishers pay a lot of money for that prime space. They are, however, poison to your state of mind. When you read the headline about that A-list actress who has put on the pounds, your mind triggers images and emotions about weight gain but not about her—about *you!* The thought "weight gain" goes out into the universe, and guess what is coming back to you? If you slip up, quickly imagine something positive. Perhaps see yourself as the slim, fit, attractive person you desire to be. But it is so much easier on your mentality to avoid looking at those gossip magazines in the first place.

6. Notice the real love all around.

Recently, I was sitting in a hotel lounge with a business associate. He watches television news avidly and, like many people, he believes that his favorite channel has no hidden agendas. We have had fun discussions about that. I point out that the owners of the channel are also one of the biggest manufacturers of war machinery and weapons in the world. He insists that if there were something to criticize about a certain foreign policy, the channel would do so. The fact that they never have and instead promote certain conflicts with catchy ticker headlines eludes him.

I have yet to find an unbiased television news channel anywhere in the world. One time, I saw the same news story presented three different ways by the same network in three regions, the United States, Europe, and Asia. Same story, same channel, but each interpretation was massaged to appeal to its audience.

A news story flashed behind me (I always sit with my back to hotel and restaurant televisions if I can), and like a cat spotting a stray mouse, his eyes locked onto the ticker tagline. Whatever it was, it made his blood boil, and he made some comments about the state of society and what we are becoming. I stopped him, and asked him to look around the lounge. I asked how many people were arguing or fighting. When he admitted there were none, I asked him how many people were holding hands, cuddling, smiling, or laughing? The answer was everyone. That is our real world. He got the point, but before long his attention snapped back to a new ticker tagline.

It is good to remind yourself that the world is not the place of disappointment, hate, and crime portrayed by the triffids. If you are one of those people obsessed with certain daytime movie channels, where all men supposedly hate women and want to hurt them, switch channels now. You can only watch a woman being physically attacked and held hostage so many times before you start making it a point to keep one hand on the pepper spray whenever a guy approaches. I have lived in man-ville for more than forty years, and I have met many more men terrified of women than the other way around!

The romantic comedy *Love Actually* has a charming introduction that makes a great point about the world around us being one of love. Voyeuristically, the camera watches people as they exit the customs area in an airport, to be greeted by friends and family. All we see are expressions of utter joy. That is the real world. No one is creeping around in fear of being victimized.

The film begins with a voiceover from Hugh Grant's character commenting that whenever he gets gloomy with the state of the world, he thinks about the arrivals terminal at Heathrow Airport and the pure uncomplicated love felt as friends and families welcome their arriving loved ones. Grant's voiceover also relates that all the known messages left by the people who died on the 9/11 planes were messages of love and not hate. The film then tells ten interrelated love stories. If the state of the world as portrayed by what you see on television has you in a depressed state, I recommend you watch this movie, then spend a few hours at an airport arrivals area.

In an airport or hotel, I take special notice of the people around me. I see laughter, love, and people caring for one another. There is an inordinate amount of hugging going on. Next time you travel, look around and see how people are behaving. That is our real world, not the one you see on a television screen.

Start today to be selective about what you watch and listen to. As much as you can, start to separate yourself from the complainers. If nothing else, remember the one subtle change in behavior is to no longer be *against* things you don't want in your life but to be *for* things you do want. That has made a huge difference in my life of mentality.

3

My Life of Mentality

WHEN I WAS TWELVE, I joined the state-run, comprehensive
high school. It was five miles from my village, but the bus
trip lasted more than an hour because it stopped at a dozen
mountain hamlets. The first day passed uneventfully until the
return ride home. Suddenly, I was yanked out of my seat by a
dozen brutal hands and dragged to the back of the bus. A gang
of bullies, all several years older than me and a good deal bigger, held me down while other kids stripped me half naked and
wrote obscenities in ballpoint pen on my torso, arms, and legs.

As bullying goes, it was humiliating but relatively harmless.
What shocked me, however, was that as a heavy knee crushed my
head into the worn fabric of a seat and I was forced to stare
down the center aisle of the bus, I saw a dozen adults, who had
spent the day shopping in the town and used the bus for free,
sitting rigidly while doing their best to pretend they couldn't
hear or see anything. Sharp pens being dragged across vulner-
able skin are painful, and they must have been able to hear me
as I struggled to free myself. Among my fellow travelers were
people from my village and half a dozen kids I thought were my
friends. No one moved. Even the bus driver, who could see all
the commotion in his rearview mirror, did nothing.

When there was no more room to write on my skin, I was allowed to return to my seat. I tuned out the chanting and laughter coming from behind. When the bus pulled up to our stop, I walked the last mile home with my sister as if nothing had happened despite the fact that several of the bullies were still jeering around me.

At home, I told my parents that the first day had gone well and then ran upstairs to the bathroom. We were poor, and I knew how hard it had been for them to afford the school uniform. I feared the bullies had torn my shirt and that I would get into big trouble for it. Fortunately, there was only minor damage. It was 1972, and Audrey was very ill at this point. The last thing our family needed was something more to worry about.

Like most kids who are victims of bullying, I felt the fault lay with me. I had been bullied at my previous two schools. In Liverpool, I was often in trouble at home for losing items of school uniform like a school blazer, cap, tie, and even a shoe. Older boys from the "posh" school stole them from me, but I was too ashamed to admit it to my parents. This time the tormenting felt systematic and more menacing than before. I believed something weak, ugly, or low about me must have caused their tribal behavior.

I stripped and tried to wash off the ink, but it was at least two weeks before the graffiti was completely gone. We did not have a shower set up in the house, and I was only able to erase the marks from my arms and stomach. As I stood in front of the mirror, I had two thoughts. The first, illogically, was about how neat the handwriting and artwork were, considering the difficulty of the bone-shaking bus ride. The second was the recurring image of everyone else working hard at looking the other way, and how united they were in their persecution, and how much like an outcast I felt.

I know now that I was targeted for two reasons. First, we were an English family living in Wales at a time when "foreigners" were not welcome. Although Wales shares a close political and social history with the rest of Great Britain, it has retained a distinct cultural identity and enjoys a degree of separate government. We had moved there four years earlier and arrived in a village where generations of the same families had always lived. The locals rarely traveled more than a few miles, and although they could speak English as well as their native tongue, they refused to do so around us. Being considered foreign, and coming from a city considered working class and with a reputation for petty crime, we were unwelcome.

In 1972, the television blared out nightly news about richer English families "invading" Wales to buy up weekend or vacation homes. The increased demand raised prices until they were well out of reach for young, native couples. Images of angry mobs torching recently purchased "outsider" homes made for compulsive viewing on the nightly bulletins. Who can tear their eyes away from newsreel of a burning house or a forest fire? A fringe political party increased the tension with their calls for the English to be ousted, Wales to be an independent nation, and their distinct and ancient language to be first choice.

It was sectarian racism, and I was targeted by the bullies on the bus with the same fervor as the television news had glorified. The fact that my family lived in an abandoned farmhouse that was barely fit for any human habitation was irrelevant to my tormentors. Their unguarded mentalities absorbed the images on television, and their habitual reaction was to act out their version of lynching on kids like me.

Second, being poor was difficult to disguise. Having odd-sized shoes of different styles on each foot was a bit of a giveaway. To make matters worse, on a Monday morning, the class teacher handed out food stamps for free school lunches to the kids whose parents were receiving welfare support. The half a dozen of us who made the long walk up to her desk under the eyes of our classmates might as well have had "untouchable" written in white chalk on the backs of our black blazers. For the simple reason that nothing unites people more than a common dislike, poor kids are also usually the victims of bullying.

My parents had received a welfare subsidy for the purchase of school uniforms, which only ran to two shirts, one tie, one blazer, a pair of trousers, and one pair of shoes. It was sufficient for most of the school year, but that first winter, the water pipes to our farmhouse froze. It was impossible to bathe properly, and we mashed snow in the bath to make water for cleaning our teeth and for Harry's shaving.

During the day at school, I was soccer mad. I ran around the playground like crazy, kicking at a tennis ball, which was the only ball I had to play with, until the school bell rang. I reluctantly returned to lessons, red-faced and sweaty. After a few days of this, and without the ability to wash my skin or clothes at home, I must have smelled like old kippers. Before long, someone taunted me about it. I reacted angrily, got in a fight, and that was like flicking a switch that united everyone else against me. Even those girls and boys who had been friendly up until then joined in the like-minded taunting.

After a few days, I learned to keep bathing materials in my locker at school. When no teachers were watching the physical education area, I ran to the changing rooms and showered quickly. I learned to play soccer with a naked torso even in the freezing weather. *Skins* we called it, and all the poor kids were first to volunteer to play on the skins team, regardless of the weather.

Kids can be cruel and geniuses at hiding things from their parents. Despite my only having the washing problem for a short time and having genuine reasons for it, I lived for years with the knowledge that the kids behind me in class or walking the corridors were making fun of me by pinching their noses and making gagging noises. Girls shunned me as if I were a leper. I remember many nights staring into the bathroom mirror under a bare lamp bulb to find what it was about me that made me so abhorrent to them.

I was not alone. Other "untouchables" were targeted for other reasons, and we just had to grin and bear it. For a while, I let the taunts impact my self-esteem, and my schoolwork deteriorated. Before that first winter, I had been the top male student. Within a few months, I had fallen to twentieth out of thirty. Below me were most of the other untouchables, all of us systematically bullied and shunned by the rest of our classmates. Candy and allowances were stolen. My blazer was ripped off my back and urinated on, and then I was forced to put it back on. When I could, I fought back. I usually won a one-on-one fistfight, but that seemed only to strengthen the group bonded against me. I felt ashamed and sure that something about me deserved the punishment.

One night in 1974, the phone rang at home. It was a rare event because the phone bill was usually unpaid, and most of the time we were without a working line. My father assumed the role of answering the phone, and we tuned into the tone of his voice. This call was clearly bad news. To my surprise, he called me to the hallway and said the call was for me. It was the headmaster, and he solemnly informed me that a classmate, Simon, one of the untouchables, had committed suicide with his father's hunting rifle. He was just thirteen, and I was stunned. The headmaster probed me to see if I had any idea why he would have done this, and I realized that he thought I was one of Simon's tormentors. Someone must have suggested it, and because we were poor and "foreign," I was a good fit. I was horrified but politely answered his questions.

Simon's death had another profound effect on me. He had been a quiet, soulful boy and immature compared to his peers. Whether bullying played a role in his death, no one could say for certain, but I was determined not to let anyone get under my skin that way. Fighting back against my tormentors had not helped, so I chose to simply keep out of everyone's way.

At that age, I was a voracious reader. The town library became a sanctuary for me, and it was a place where I was treated as an equal and where my status in society and shabby clothes went unnoticed. None of the bullies were ever likely to cause me trouble there. At lunchtimes and on Saturdays, whenever I was not playing soccer, I would spend hours in the library reference department, where I discovered a whole section of biographies of famous and self-made men and women. The first one hooked me, and after that I became an addict.

The librarians got to know me and my taste in books and suggested many an inspiring read. I do not remember all their names, but their dedication and help has always been appreciated. With the launch of this book, I am donating a free copy to every library in the United States. Hopefully, *Three Simple Steps* will end up in the hands of a kid like I was and be an inspiration to take control of his or her destiny.

If you are a kid reading this sentence right now, understand that you are full of unlimited potential. No one can determine your path but you, and everything you want is possible. Learn to control your mentality, and you will succeed. In a bizarre way, being an outcast can teach you the power of individualism, and that can be the foundation of a self-made life. If you are being bullied, consider reading biographies of successful people such as Ranulph Fiennes so you can learn how others turned their situations into what made them successful.

Sir Ranulph Fiennes is an adventurer and holder of several endurance records. He served in the Army for eight years including a period on counter-insurgency service while attached to the army of the Sultanate of Oman. He later undertook numerous expeditions and was the first person to visit both the

North and South Poles by surface means and the first to cross Antarctica on foot. In May 2009, at the age of 65, he climbed to the summit of Mount Everest. According to the *Guinness Book of World Records*, he is the world's greatest living explorer. One would assume that he would have been first to be recruited to any boy's gang. As a child, however, this "man's man" struggled at the hands of bullies:

> Such remorseless nastiness squeezed every last trace of self-confidence from me. At one point, I stood on Windsor Bridge and contemplated throwing myself off. I didn't go through with it, but I can understand why some children feel so bad that they think about suicide. It lasted for about two years . . . Looking back, I can see that Eton inadvertently built *individualism*. You either conformed or realized there was no way you could conform. Once you realized you could not conform, *it strengthened your ability to be an individual.*

Other famous people who have described the torment of bullying and how they overcame it include Bill Gates, Steve Jobs, Michael Phelps, Pierce Brosnan, Christina Aguilera, Tom Cruise, Kristen Stewart, Winona Ryder, and Sandra Bullock. They are all *individuals* who learned the power of controlling their mentalities to become successful.

Although the library became my safe haven, I was fascinated to read about the lives of people who had far more to overcome than I did. I was inspired by their unshakeable belief in their individualism and how they refused to conform to the common thinking of their time. Most of them described mental and physical tricks that they used to shut out the world that screamed at them, and many of the men and women in the books shared one technique in particular. Then I saw it being used on television, and I gave it a go myself.

In the mid-1970s, I enjoyed watching golf and tennis tournaments on TV. I think it was the isolation of the player and the fact that it is one person against the opponent, the course, the crowd, and the critics that kept my attention on those particular sports. I loved watching sports stars who were unmoved by the hostility in the crowds around them. Men like Björn Borg and Jack Nicklaus were heroes to me. Sevvy Ballesteros had turned professional at just sixteen years old. Now, here was a kid half Jack Nicklaus's age and only a year older than me, playing alongside him with the same implacable calm.

After a successful round, the interviewer asked Ballesteros how he coped with the pressure of playing with such icons and with the raucous crowd that followed them. Politely, he explained that he came from a family of gifted golfers, and he had been taught a technique whereby he imagined a thick glass jar descending from the sky and covering him completely. Inside his glass jar, he said, he was able to shut out the outside world, stay centered, and achieve anything.

The interviewer seemed uninterested and went on to ask more mundane tournament-related questions. I literally jumped out of my chair with excitement. Although it used modernized imagery, his technique was the same one I had read about in many biographies. Some called it a deflection spell; others called it a mental shield.

Everyday thereafter, I walked to the school bus stop using a different route than my siblings. This required climbing a fence, crossing a muddy field, and rejoining them half a mile away. They probably thought I was in a grumpy teenage mood. What I actually did during that detour, however, was to imagine that a huge glass cloak descended from the sky and completely covered me as I walked. By the time I rejoined my siblings, I was fully protected inside this shield. I imagined all slurs and taunts bouncing off the glass or exploding on impact.

The effect of this simple trick was astounding. I felt powerful and impervious to any insults. No one could hurt me anymore. My schoolwork returned to its higher standard. I played better at sports. For the first time in my life, girls seemed willing to interact with me. It was as if someone had flicked a switch, and I had changed my persona overnight. Gradually, my self-esteem improved. I gained confidence and, perhaps because I was no longer focusing on it and certainly no longer *against* it, the bullying simply stopped.

Then in 1976, Sevvy Ballesteros came in second in the British Open and captured the world's attention. I watched his performance, and true to his interview, he was so calm under pressure. I have used this technique ever since, a trick I call my *mentality shield.* Whether in investor meetings, public speaking, or just in a crowd at a concert, it protects me from external stimuli that I don't want in my mind. Over the years, I have studied a wide variety of religions and disciplines and I find a form of my mentality shield in all of them.

In the same year Ballesteros achieved fame, it was time for me to choose a career. University was not an option I ever considered because we were poor. England did not have the retail and restaurant infrastructure of America, so working one's way through university was not an option and scholarships were not as available back then.

All of my ancestors had served in the military, and many had experienced the horrors of war. My father had been in the Royal Air Force, and his father had served in the army. Growing up in the farmhouse, military service was certainly glorified. Prints of fighter planes and bombers adorned the walls. The fire utensils were held in empty ammunition shell-cases. We played in the loft with old gas masks and tin helmets. Plastic models of planes and tanks were the common birthday or Christmas gifts handed out. I had dozens of them. We watched any television movie or drama that had to do with the war, and there were lots of them through the sixties and seventies.

When friends and relatives visited, the conversation turned to the war years within minutes. They were all brought up similarly, and their like-mindedness reinforced their beliefs. Seated at the dinner table, I lapped up every story. It all sounded like a great adventure. Years of external stimuli had rewired my neurons sufficiently so that I never really considered any career option other than the military. My siblings were similarly wired and joined the Royal Air Force when they turned sixteen. I don't think they ever considered an alternative.

Every Sunday, so long as the utility bill and weekly television rental fee had been paid, Audrey and I looked forward to watching a program called *Holiday*. It is the longest running travel review show in the United Kingdom, and in the mid-1970s, it was at its peak. Audrey had never traveled farther than the shoreline. Harry's only trip overseas was a military deployment to Egypt. For the poor, a holiday abroad was a distant dream, and we looked on with a mix of fascination and envy. I wanted nothing more than to be able to see some of those exotic places one day.

I figured I could at least get to see some of the world as well as have a career if I joined the Royal Navy. A documentary series called *Sailor* was a big television hit at the same time. The camera followed some young officers as they struggled to build their early naval careers. Their lives seemed so glamorous and so far removed from my own as they traveled to all kinds of exotic locations. I decided that was what I wanted to do.

Everyone but Audrey laughed at me. No one in our family history had ever been "officer class." In the 1970s, the military academies were elitist, and the Royal Naval College had produced a high percentage of the country's political leaders. Only the sons of titled people were typically admitted.

When I mentioned it to the school career advisor, she pointed out that no one from the province where we lived had ever been admitted to an officer academy in any of the military branches. Instead, she showed me a brochure of a chicken-packing plant in the next town and suggested I apply for an apprenticeship. Fortunately, I was wearing my mentality shield that day and gently deflected her offer.

People around me were quick to point out that I hardly offered the appropriate school or family connections, and my accent clearly marked me as lower class. Everyone thought I was stepping above my station, and I think most were worried that I was setting myself up for a fall.

The radio blasted the latest doom and gloom about the economy, which was decimated in the mid-1970s in the United Kingdom. Military commanders were threatening to quit because of the severe budget cutbacks. The Royal Navy announced it was cutting two thousand positions.

Fortunately for me, I never listened to the radio news. In my spare time, I was always outdoors or down at the library. Despite never having any money and not once succeeding at any venture, my father was obsessed with business and financial news. When he turned up the volume to listen to a talking head tell how bad the state of affairs had become, I went for a walk in the woods. I was not smart enough at the time to know I was protecting my mentality. I just preferred to be outdoors. It probably saved me because I never let any outside influence dilute my dream of becoming a naval officer.

Pestered enough, a parent will break in the face of a child's insistence. Realizing I would not let go of the desire, Audrey made an appointment for me to visit the Royal Navy recruiting offices in a town thirty miles away. Despite the pain in her bones from the cancer, she insisted on making the trip with me. She put on her best outfit and I wore my school uniform, but we still looked ragged.

Three bus routes and a long, painful walk through town later, we arrived at the intimidating building. A tall, fit-looking officer stood behind a huge oak desk as we entered the meeting room. He was in full uniform, sword at his side. When he spoke, his eloquence startled me. I felt my mother shrink back as we took seats opposite the desk.

The officer looked down his nose, took in Audrey's thread-bare outfit and while still standing, pronounced the following sentence, which even to this day I recall word for word: "Her Majesty's Royal Navy always applauds ambition. However, I feel it only fair to inform you that we have, how may one put it delicately, certain standards. It would be quite wrong to raise this young man's hopes."

My mother blushed, and I wanted to punch him for humiliating her. I stood to leave, but Audrey's firm hand set me back in a seat. Her eyes bore into the officer, and he had to look away. She insisted he give me an application form. The man made a token protest, but my mother stared him into submission. Years before, I had seen her put God in his place, so I began to feel sorry for this mere mortal. I doubt he had faced enemies in battle more determined than Audrey was in that moment.

Sometime after that trip, I was in a classroom when the teacher began asking if everyone had made their minds up about careers or universities. When I stated that I had applied to join the Royal Navy College, the teacher choked back a laugh. Several of my classmates tittered. The teacher made some comment about there being a fine line between ambition and arrogance. I was no longer bothered by other people's opinions, so added no more explanation. I had started to develop that unshakeable belief in my ability that I had read about in the lives of so many self-made people.

Two months later, when everyone but me had forgotten about the trip to the recruiting office, a letter from the Admiralty arrived.

It stated that my application had been accepted. I was invited to the Admiralty Interview Board in London to be tested mentally and physically. Most people we knew were shocked by it and quick to point out that it was probably a token gesture. Some said it was a politically correct move so the military authorities could not be accused of bias against people from working-class families under our new socialist government.

Having never been away from home before, it was a daunting prospect for a sixteen-year-old. Audrey ordered a suit for me from a catalogue that offered weekly payment terms. It was a gray pinstripe with flared trousers and I looked like I was either going to a wedding or a Valentine's Day massacre. I made the trip alone by train and bus.

Everyone else who had been invited to the tests was older than me, and I was the only one with a working-class accent. I realized, however, that the perceived prejudice was in my mind only. I had been brought up to believe in the class divide, but at the Admiralty, everyone treated me as an equal. I made fast friendships and have fond memories of that week. I had no idea how I performed, but I gave it everything.

I realized quickly that the tests were about character. Some of them seemed designed to cause the candidate to fail, and I noticed quite a few had a hard time with not being able to complete their tasks. I had control of my mentality by then and I understood that the test was not about winning but about remaining calm under pressure. With my mentality shield in place, staying unflappable was now second nature. After every question or challenge thrown my way, I would pause before choosing how to react. I mapped my mind ever so carefully out on my tongue.

Months went by with no response from the Admiralty. Everyone around me either tried to console me or tease me about not making it. Out of the blue, a second letter from the

Admiralty arrived. Because I was not yet of age, it was addressed to my father, and we all gathered in the lounge as he read out my sentence in a formal manner. I had been accepted to the college and, in addition, had been offered a rare scholarship.

Two years later, when I was the appropriate age, I entered the naval college as a midshipman. Joining me in the line of arrivals at the college in 1979 and wearing the largest name badge I had ever seen, was *His Royal Highness—The Midshipman—Prince Andrew*, the middle son of Queen Elizabeth II—someone I had only seen before in news footage. He looked even more nervous than I felt. Quite unnecessarily, he introduced himself. We shook hands, but I was so unprepared, I could not think of a thing to say. I think I just grunted. I do, however, remember wondering what that recruitment officer would have made of the scene.

To have been transported from the derelict farmhouse to the higher echelons of the Naval College is in itself a rags-to-riches story that's the stuff of fairy tales. The success was purely down to my decision to control my mentality. I was beginning to feel that I could do anything, but I still had the daunting prospect of surviving military training, which had a notoriously high drop-out rate.

Military officer training is a proven process of character building. From beginning to end, the intention is to form new mentalities and to mold everyone into the like-mindedness of the required style and standard. Orders have to be given and obeyed without deliberation. It is indoctrination, but not so different from the way our mentalities are formed in civilian life. The differences are that the recruits are fully aware and eager for it to happen, and the time constraints intensify the process.

I realized early on that our backgrounds didn't matter at all. The process was to crush every ego to dust, and then rebuild characters quickly according to some traditional blueprint. That intensity makes the process necessarily brutal. At times, sleep, nourishment, and even time to breathe are luxuries. I found, however, that being in control of my mentality was a great advantage. I let nothing anyone said or did shake me from my intention of succeeding. When I screwed up and was bawled out by a senior officer, it did not bother me like it did others. I recognized the process for what it was, and most of the time I was wearing my mentality shield anyway.

From thousands of applicants, several hundred were invited to the Admiralty interviewing process, and only one hundred made it from there to the college. Two years later, only five of us were left to graduate. Along the way, people were rejected when they failed academically. There were no second chances. Some could not take the physical or mental regimen and left of their own accord. The majority simply had not been tested beyond their known endurance before, and their characters failed them at crucial times.

An unexpected benefit of the physical side to the training was that I became much fitter. Being an outdoors type as a kid and a decent amateur-standard soccer player, I was already in reasonable shape. The Navy's training, however, added muscular strength and stamina. Before long, I broke into the soccer first-team squad. On my debut in an away game against an army base, I scored the winner in a 2–1 victory and never looked back after that. A month later, I was chosen to play on a navy select team that was to tour military bases in Germany and Holland.

I was nineteen but had never been in an airport or stepped on a plane. All I knew of the countries was what I had seen on those *Holiday* programs on television that I watched with my mother. Finally, I was getting to live my dream of travel. What everyone had said was impossible was now my reality. I was traveling around Europe, while playing the game I loved, and with the glamour and salary of being a naval officer. I didn't think life could get much better.

Every military branch has its equivalent of the "week of hell," a harsh survival and endurance course designed to test anyone to the limit. My test came at the end of the first year and we were airlifted to a bleak mountain in the middle of a snowy December.

After route marching for the third day in a row without much sleep or food while carrying equipment that was deliberately weighted down with wet sand, I saw grown men cry. Every few miles, a mental or logistics test awaited us. It was as diverse as building a bridge out of the equipment to cross an impossibly swollen river or walking naked through an almost frozen lake to get clothes and equipment across without letting them get wet.

The worst torture is the offer to end the endurance. All day and all night, our transmitters blared at regular intervals with offers of a warm bed and food if we were only to ask for it. Anonymity was assured, and each morning our group got smaller. During the night, several always left quietly and without prejudice. I never saw them again.

In that week, five of our group suffered exposure and were airlifted off the mountain. Two broke bones. One collapsed, claiming not to be able to move another inch. Although it was explicitly against the rules, we carried him and his equipment for the next two days until he was removed from the exercise on health grounds. We also had to carry the equipment of all those who had left for any reason.

At night, we slept for a few uneasy hours under a tarpaulin. Our breath froze on the inside of the tarp so that it took all our remaining strength to fold it up small enough to carry. Just as REM sleep arrived, an explosion, or a megaphone would always rouse us and we would have to break camp.

Sleep deprivation is a known method of torture and I lost all sense of place and time. My feet were so blistered that they looked reptilian. Yet inside my mind, I felt calm and confident. The outside world ceased to have form or meaning. It was just a matter of taking one more step, then another.

When I finally reached the target destination after eight days with my few remaining colleagues, we were a day later than expected. I assumed the other groups had made it safely and were back at the college in the dry and warmth. The receiving officer, who was not too pleased to have been made to wait another day in that bleak landscape, informed us that our group was the only one to make the destination.

I often think about that week, and I try to find some common denominator in those who survived, and in those who gave up. There is nothing obvious. One was the son of a Right Honorable politician. He was fit, well spoken, and a hit with the ladies. One was a vicar's only child, mild-mannered and introverted. One was the pragmatic son of a senior police commissioner. We were all different shapes and sizes, some more academically talented than others, all from completely different backgrounds and upbringings. None of us had ever been tested like that before. During the whole week, however, we all had an unshakeable belief that we would make the destination. None of us ever doubted it, and we never had to encourage each other.

We encouraged the others in our group, tried hard to talk them out of quitting, and carried more than our loads to give them a break. When the snow became a blizzard, we walked faster. When the pains in our empty stomachs caused some to double up in agony, we started singing. Whatever stimuli smacked our mentalities, we carefully chose our reactions. I believe that is why we made it to the destination. It is the only thing we had in common. We controlled our reactions to the extreme situations around us.

After a couple days to recover, I was called to the Captain's office. As I expected, we had been followed and monitored every step of the way by seasoned special troops. Our conversations had been recorded, and a report had been compiled on our performance under duress. It was like that all the time. Officers are constantly being assessed, inside and outside the college. The report was fair, and I had been assessed with average marks. The Captain told me that there was something in the assessment to indicate potential leadership skills, but he wanted to test some more. Just like that, I was promoted, not on merit, but as a test; the next morning I found myself in charge of a division of forty people.

I was still in the character-forming phase of my training and had developed no leadership skills or talent that could make me useful as a divisional leader. I was nineteen but with a baby face that made me still look like a schoolboy. Yet there I was with yellow bands on my uniform, addressing a room full of older, hardened personnel. Just like back at the high school, I was aware of the whispers behind my back from the veterans who thought me too green to succeed.

I was given a book of standing orders and personnel reports with a summary of the divisional performance. It was so much information to digest, that I mostly just scanned the pages. Even doing that, it was obvious that the division had issues. Out of five divisions, their performances placed them fourth, but historically they had regularly been at the top, and the hierarchy was not happy.

When I addressed the room, I could feel everyone's tension. Initially, I was not sure how they would accept such a young, inexperienced leader, but I saw in their eyes a complete lack of confidence, not in me but in themselves. It felt as if they were ashamed. I realized that they needed someone to encourage them. They did not care so much who I was, where I was from, or how old I was, so long as I could help them look good again.

Initially, there was some complaining and finger-pointing, and everyone had a desire to analyze what was going wrong. Their mentalities were *against* many things, including their failures. In reading the biographies of great men and women, many attributed their success to being able to cut through the detail of complicated projects and focus on key points. Men like Henry Ford and Andrew Carnegie ran businesses for which they had no qualifications or history. Then they would hire experts in each key area to form a tight group of functional leaders. They also shunned too much analysis on the past for a focus more on what the company desired to achieve. Those tycoons were always *for* something. I used the same idea.

I broke the divisional tasks down to its three key elements of logistics, engineering, and seamanship. Then I read through personnel reports to find people who could be the expert functional leaders. Some of them took a lot of cajoling, but I encouraged them to follow my approach and break their function down to its three core elements, and recruit experts in each task, all the while encouraging each task leader to break their task down into its three core technical details and recruit skilled people to perform them, etc. I had no idea how to do any of the things I was asking them to do because I had yet to be trained for them.

I stopped the downward spiral of what everyone was *against* and got them thinking about what they were *for*, which was to be the best division again. To be the best, each had to be the best in his role, either as a functional leader or a technical worker. It was a success, and within six months the division was ranked number one in all parameters.

All of the hard work was done by functional and task leaders. All I did was change their mentalities a little. At no time was I popular because it was a new approach and a lot of hard work. I was not used to leadership and realize now that I was not at all flexible or considerate of feelings at the time. I was told by one of my peers that I was even the subject of restroom wall graffiti for my strict discipline in the turnaround. I was not there to win friends, however; I was there to win. The cynics in the division did their best to disrupt the program, but I was able to shut out their negative energy sufficiently to focus on what we were aiming for. Without even knowing it back then, I was becoming a master of my mentality.

The benefits of this success paid off almost immediately. Suddenly, the hierarchy saw promise in this pauper made good. I started to get my pick of assignments, and I chose anything that meant travel. I spent six weeks as a guest of the British Embassy in Paris. I took command of a picket boat and sailed up the Rivers Seine and Marne. I spent two weeks as a guest of a famous champagne family at their chateau. On my first trip at sea, I visited Cyprus, Turkey, Malta, Italy, Madeira, Gibraltar, Greece, and Africa.

I got to play soccer in every country and made many foreign friends. All the time, I kept reminding myself that if I had not controlled my mentality, I would have let others talk me out of this adventure before it began. I could see the power of mentality control with every step I took. I remember a gloriously sunny day in January, standing on the flat-topped rock that holds the Acropolis of Athens, 500 feet above sea level, and thinking to myself, "I did this. I made this happen."

That ability to control mentality was soon to have its hardest test. After I graduated, with the award of college colors, two experiences combined to change my life quickly. Both shocked me. Having been so immersed in my adventure, I had given little thought to the outside world. For the graduation ceremony, I had arranged to meet my parents at a local hotel. I walked straight by Audrey without recognizing her. In the time since I had last been home on leave, her cancer had worsened. She looked like a wizened old lady, barely able to hobble along with the aid of walking sticks. Not only was the sight of her a shock, I was stunned that I had become so self-involved with the navy project that I really had given her condition very little thought. It was like a slap in the face.

After the ceremony, I took compassionate leave, and on the first day that I took her to the hospital for her chemotherapy, the second experience slapped me even harder. I saw my future wife and fell head over heels in love.

My leave lasted six weeks before the navy started to insist that I return. I had been assigned a terrific job at sea on the newest frigate. My four fellow graduates were green with envy. In those six weeks, however, something had changed inside me. I realized I was intoxicated by the travel and glamour, but not necessarily dedicated to the service as much as I should be. Instinctively, I knew I would resign my commission, because the navy demands that it become your mother, wife, and family. There can be no half measures or partial commitments.

Even during my brief naval life, I had seen so many servicemen suffer broken hearts while away on duty. The "Dear John" letters, as we called them, happened every week. The thought of my mother dying while I was away, after all she had done for me, was too much. Additionally, I couldn't get the image of my future wife out of my head. I knew I was going to marry her. It is impossible to explain that feeling, but for any cynics reading this, I can tell you for a fact that love at first sight is as real as the American dream. Don't let anyone try to tell you different.

After weeks of sleepless nights, and with my bosses heaping pressure on me to return, I made my decision. I told no one else for fear that they would try to talk me out of it and traveled down to the port as normal. Everyone from my ex-teachers, my family, and friends, to the local newspaper reporter were now following my career. The pressure of letting all those people down weighed heavily. The train journey passed while I was in a trance-like state.

Aboard the frigate, the Captain tried his hardest to talk me out of my decision. He was so sure of the mistake I was making that he broke the strict rules and let me read my career performance reports. In one was a wonderful line that commented on the strength of my *mentality*. I had to smile. I almost cracked. I was seconds away from changing my mind, but I resigned my commission.

I was bombarded by criticism from all quarters. People's biggest concern seemed to be their fear that I was following the same pattern of behavior as my father and his father. Some of the rhetoric was vitriolic.

No one stopped yelling at me long enough to allow me to explain, and I learned another important lesson with regard to control of mentality. One of the harder things to accept when it comes to taking control of your destiny is that sometimes the only way to stop the negative external stimuli is to shut it off. That is easy when it comes to a television or radio but hard when it comes to people. Some people were so persistent in their criticism that, for my own sanity, I had to shut them down. A phone call cut short or an unanswered letter, and those people exited my life forever. It would not be the last time I had to do that, but it is always hard to let go.

Over the next few months, I continued to take Audrey to the hospital for her chemotherapy appointments, but it took me a long time to conjure up the courage to ask my future wife on a date. A few weeks before Audrey died, she asked me, "Is she the one?" I did not need to answer. She smiled, and whispered, "I'm glad."

■ ■ ■

This is the conclusion of Step One. This step needs to be the first to be mastered because, to escape the quicksand, you need to start thinking and reacting according to your own instincts. It is the way to rediscover the pioneering spirit with which you were born. Intentionally or otherwise, the media and people in your environment wire your neurons in a like-minded manner, unless you consciously start to change that process. The changes are simple, but not easy, because you must consistently control your mentality.

With the gentle encouragement of my publisher, I have revealed intimate details about my life that many of my friends and family will read for the first time. I am an intensely private person and this was an uncomfortable process, but necessary. So many self-help books are written by people who don't practice what they teach, and the writers have often not encountered success before their book starts selling well. That lack of credibility has always bothered me. Authenticity is essential if this book is to be of real value to you, and that necessitates it being so personal. Parts of my life story are the best testimony to the power of these principles.

If you start to make small changes in your thoughts and reactions, you will get out of your version of quicksand. I did, and I am no different than anyone else.

Step Two shows you what to do once you are out of the quicksand. In all those autobiographies I have read, what separates the successful from the crowd is a winning idea. Step Two shows you how to rewire your neurons to put yourself in a position to have those moments of insight.

PART TWO

STAYING OUT OF THE QUICKSAND

Creating Winning Ideas

A human being is a part of a whole, called by us "universe," a part limited in time and space. He experiences himself, his thoughts and feelings as something separated from the rest . . . a kind of optical delusion of his consciousness. This delusion is a kind of prison for us, restricting us to our personal desires and to affection for a few persons nearest to us. Our task must be to free ourselves from this prison by widening our circle of compassion to embrace all living creatures and the whole of nature in its beauty.

ALBERT EINSTEIN, 1954

WHEN EINSTEIN WAS WORKING on his theories, the scientific community believed in the relativity principle, which had been formulated centuries earlier by Galileo. This principle was incomplete and Einstein was obsessed with its flaws—so much so that he tortured his mind with it for a full *ten* years.

It became his life. He spoke of nothing else, discussed it endlessly with other scientists, and challenged friends with the riddle of what happens to space and time at the speed of light. It was the last thing he contemplated before sleep and the first thing he thought of when he awoke. The answer eluded him and he got stuck in the quicksand with his scientific buddies.

Einstein rarely slept more than a few hours. To compensate, he started taking what he called "meditative naps" during the day. After one of these naps, he is said to have jumped out of his chair with an idea that changed the course of civilization.

In 1905, he published his conclusion in a three-page paper titled "Does the Inertia of a Body Depend on Its Energy Content?" The paper had neither footnotes nor a single reference to support it. The scientific community vilified him for twenty years until technology became available to validate his moment of insight.

Every week, I meet people who tell me that they want a better life, but they just don't have any good ideas about how to change things. As hard as they try, they can't find a solution. Step Two of the three simple steps has many benefits for your life. Most, however, are beyond the scope of this book and are well documented elsewhere. We are interested in one aspect of this step, which is all about positioning yourself to create and respond to good ideas.

In my experience of teaching the three simple steps, most people readily accept the common sense of controlling mentality in Step One. Those who take it to heart experience dramatic improvements in their lives. Those who take it lightly still enjoy many benefits. Step Three, which is about how to execute great ideas to create anything you want, gets people excited. Most people, however, skip Step Two, or if they attempt Step Two, they do so for a while and then forget about it. That's because we are brought up in a society where focusing outward is acceptable but looking inward is associated with being esoteric.

When Steve Jobs, the cofounder of Apple Inc., passed away in 2011, in the majority of obituaries that made front-page news, the journalists waxed lyrical about his brilliant mind, his micromanagement style of leadership, and the impact his inventions had on the modern world. The fact he left college to travel around India, where he found and converted to Buddhism, and then spent the rest of his days as a practicing Buddhist, meditating every day, was almost always a throwaway line. It was as if they were saying he was 95 percent normal, and it is okay to allow him 5 percent weird. After all, it did not harm the impact he made or the success he had.

Instead, they should be connecting the dots between his passions for meditation and being with nature, both of which are scientifically proven to improve brain function, and the runaway success of his business and life.

In Step One, we discussed how positive vs. negative thoughts impact the neural networks, and then how exposure to prolonged stress could destroy neurons. In Step Two, we will discuss the rewiring of neural networks into a configuration that enhances our ability to create winning ideas and moments of insight.

To overcome the natural tendency for people to ignore the inner journey as something for weirdos or new-agers, I will provide solid evidence from cutting-edge neuroscience. Today, people seem to need proof to get over the fence and give it a go. For me, I always felt if it worked for Carnegie, Emerson, and Einstein, who am I to say it is not for me? At one time, I was desperate for good ideas to get me out of the quicksand. I found Step Two had a profound impact in all aspects of my life, and it is no coincidence that my wonderful adventure started the same time that I was introduced to it.

As a businessman, the thing I hear most often is comments such as "I wish I could start my own thing, but I don't have any good ideas." Just last night, a friend who strikes me as having the common sense, drive, and customer focus to be successful with his own "thing" was lamenting how much he detested his job. I asked him why he doesn't start his own company. He said he would love to, but he doesn't have any brilliant ideas about what sort of company to start.

The truth is that you don't have to come up with an idea. They are already there. Brilliant ideas, or moments of insight, are literally bursting to get through our closed-off minds. Unfortunately, the way we have learned to behave has wired our neurons in such a way that we often are oblivious to them. In the stories of successful men and women, and later through trial and error in my own life, I discovered a simple step that is designed purely to rewire neurons such that they can be receptive to those ideas again. The step is effortless. Whether you are five years old or eighty-five, you can introduce Step Two into your life right now and enjoy success, because a single moment of insight is worth a lifetime of experience.

4

A Matter of Stillness

SHORTLY AFTER AUDREY'S FUNERAL in 1982, Harry was evicted from the farmhouse when it was revealed he had not paid the £15-a-month rent for several years. The owners had resisted taking action while Audrey was ill. It was the third time in his adult life that Harry had suffered the humiliation of eviction from his home.

A trail of debts unraveled. Money had been stolen, vehicles rented and abandoned, and goods purchased on sale or return terms that were never returned. The children took responsibility for the mess, in and out of courts, over two difficult years.

Eventually, Harry's whereabouts were tracked to a damp, windowless studio that was built into a wall of a railway bridge. A naked bulb hung from frayed wires that were illegally connected to an electric conduit under the bridge. The floor was bare concrete, and the only furniture was an unmade folding bed against one wall. When I walked into the room, Harry was heating a can of soup over a Bunsen burner, his ever-present cigarette dangling from his lips. He looked up. "Hello, son," he muttered, as if he had been expecting me at that very moment.

The look of shame in his eyes hit me with the power of a sledgehammer. I had seen that look once before. As a child, I watched when Harry's father was forced by debt to close his small cake shop and move into a two-room home provided by welfare. I recalled the same expression of embarrassment. It was as if they had lived the same lives, and when I thought about it, their patterns of behavior were frighteningly similar.

In 1914, the British government launched a massive campaign to manipulate the mentalities of young men to make them join the army. "Your Country Needs You" was the slogan pasted to every wall. Lord Kitchener led a cleverly controlled exercise in guilt throwing. "Surely you will fight for your country. Come along boys before it is too late" sang the catchphrase from megaphones at every town hall. From platforms and stages, pretty girls offered any young man who agreed to sign up a kiss and a King's sovereign.

A million young men with unguarded mentalities reacted habitually. Among them, George Frederick, my grandfather, stepped up onto that stage and got his first kiss. The minimum age for joining the army was nineteen, but there was no age verification system. When he headed for the trenches, George was a gangly sixteen-year-old choirboy, barely strong enough to aim a rifle.

In 1916, at the battle of the Somme, George was one of the few survivors of his regiment when he received a second kiss in the form of a sniper's bullet to the head. He survived but was blinded. Behind the lines, he was retrained to be a cook working from a Braille recipe book. Six months later, he recovered his eyesight and was immediately moved back to the front line.

In 1917, at the third battle of Ypres, the Germans launched artillery shells containing mustard gas. They exploded short of the British trenches, releasing a gray-green fog that crept slowly toward George's position. George had not been issued a gas mask. He knew running was futile, as the second wave of artillery was always aimed to detonate on those in retreat. George made a choice to die with his boots on, a decision that saved his life.

Mustard gas was not an effective killer. It was designed to creep into the soil, making trenches uninhabitable for weeks. Exposed skin blistered. It could cause blindness, vomiting, and internal bleeding.

Unfortunately, the soldiers didn't realize that the gas was denser nearer to the ground. Those who lay down never got up again. Standing at his post, George suffered bronchial injury, but he lived. At nineteen, he returned home as a weakened man with a permanent cough.

After the war, he worked on the railways as a ticket collector, but his disabilities caused by the gassing meant he could only work part-time. His lungs were damaged, and he coughed up phlegm constantly, a habit that caused him issues at home and work, although it did nothing to slow down his cigarette smoking. After the war, he was a restless spirit, and bounced from one job to another, trying his hand at insurance sales and shopkeeping.

In 1928, he married Emily. The following year, they had their only child, Harry, and moved into a terraced house that backed onto a railway line. While Emily sold insurance to keep a roof over their heads, George opened a fruit and vegetable shop that never made any profit. When World War II arrived in 1939, rationing closed the shop.

During World War II, George volunteered as an Air Raid Warden. After the war ended for the British, in 1945, he moved to the Welsh countryside, and opened a candy shop in a small market town. When it closed, he tried a cake shop nearby, while living in a damp cottage with outside plumbing. Eventually, he retired to state-provided housing a few miles walk from our derelict farmhouse. George spent his days indoors, smoking cigarettes and reading library books, until his weakened heart caught up with him in 1971.

Harry grew up hearing first-hand accounts of war, and then experiencing the drama of World War II as a teenager. For a while, he was sent away from the city to live with strangers in the countryside where it was safer. He left as a boy and returned to his parents when he was nearly an adult. When he was eighteen, in 1947, he joined the Royal Air Force and served abroad for two years. When he returned, he landed a secure job working as a bank teller. There, he met and fell in love with Audrey.

As restless as his father, Harry left the bank to start a business of his own as a market-stall holder, first selling fruit and vegetables. When that failed, he turned his hand to making and selling furniture wholesale. He moved his family to a flat above a shop next to a busy railway line and signal control box. Escaping creditors, he moved his family once more to an isolated village in the Welsh countryside.

He initially found work as a van driver, delivering packaged meat products to shops around the region. When that ended, he sold insurance and then soft drinks from the back of a car. Throughout the 1970s, Harry started and failed at several businesses, varying from opening a tire depot to distributing wine. They rarely lasted more than a few months. His most ironic venture was a financial services company in which he advised people on their investments, mortgages, and savings, none of which he had ever experienced.

He lost his small investments and the life savings of those gullible enough to join his schemes. Eventually, he gave up trying to do anything at all and spent his days indoors while smoking cigarettes and reading library books, just like George.

The pattern in behavior and experiences between George and Harry bothered me. Finding him in that state of shame under the railway bridge made me consider my own behavior. We were alike in many ways, especially in our love of reading, and had I not also recently left a secure, promising position for an uncertain future? I knew then that I needed to be sure to avoid the ancestral repetition.

Shortly after finding Harry in that nearly homeless state under the railway bridge, I came across Napoleon Hill's famous book, *Think and Grow Rich*. This book has sold millions of copies since its publication in 1937, and many people credit it for helping them get out of their personal quicksand. I had, however, already read the detailed biographies of many of the tycoons he interviewed and drawn my own, and quite different, conclusions about what it took to succeed.

Reviewers and "how to get wealthy" bloggers describe Napoleon Hill in saintly terms: *born into poverty . . . began his writing career at age thirteen to make money . . . dedicated more than twenty-five years of his life to define the reasons by which so many people fail to achieve true financial success and happiness in their lives.* At the risk of being accused of heresy by the self-help success movement, that is not an accurate portrayal of a man who was more like George and Harry than any of the tycoons he interviewed.

Hill's grandfather was a printer, and his father became a self-taught dentist, having made an improvised and illegal set of false teeth for Hill's stepmother. His stepmother bought him a typewriter when he was thirteen, in exchange for him giving up his six-shooter and the wild life that went with it. With that typewriter, he became a reporter for the local mountain news.

There was no evidence of poverty or oppression in his childhood. He got a job with a prominent lawyer who also owned a coal mine. When the mine manager got drunk and accidentally shot a bellhop, Hill arranged to have the death covered up as an accident, using his own money to bribe the coroner. His reward was to be made manager of the mine at the age of only nineteen.

He played around with the idea of becoming a lawyer, but he let that go in favor of a partnership in a lumberyard in 1905. In 1908, Hill was wiped out when the lumberyard went belly-up. So he took himself off to New York to rebuild his life and to be in close proximity to the giants of American business and industry. Among them was seventy-four-year-old Andrew Carnegie.

The story goes that Andrew Carnegie told him to interview the wealthiest men in America and write the secrets of their success in a book, which would be "one of the most enlightening documents ever written." Carnegie did not offer to finance the project as some reviewers suggest, but he did apparently provide him with letters of introduction to fellow tycoons.

To put bread on the table, he taught advertising at the La Salle Extension University in Chicago. He then left to cofound the Betsy Ross Candy Company. He fell out with his partners, who had him tried for fraud. The judge vindicated Hill.

Over the next decade, Hill won and lost businesses, business partners (who sometimes ended up in jail), and his family's love. Controversies of some sort always seemed to accompany the loss of one of Hill's businesses. One of the governing rules he discovered was that whatever you set your heart on, you must be prepared to pay a price for, a rule contrary to my own experiences.

Despite his lack of success, Hill started a success magazine called *Hill's Golden Rule*, but eventually it also failed. He founded another periodical that featured ads for Hill-conceived organizations like the Peptomists and the Co-Operative Club. Failed again.

In 1928, Andrew Pelton, the book distributor and former advertiser in Hill's old magazine, rescued him from poverty and obscurity. Hill borrowed money, rented a hotel suite, and bought expensive cigars, which he handed out liberally amongst hotel staff. In addition to that, he tipped the bellboys heavily and dressed to kill. Every worker in the hotel viewed him as the big man. Pelton attended the meeting in the hotel. Hill was well aware Pelton would pick up on the reverence the staff showed him. It worked. Hill pitched his idea to Pelton and showed him a couple of pages of the impending book, and a deal was done right there and then. An advance on royalties was handed over on the spot.

Hill produced an eight-volume *Law of Success*, which set down his fifteen principles. The fact he had not actually discovered how to succeed in anything at this point eluded the readers, and soon he was raking in royalties of $2,500 a month. His success was writing a book about how to succeed. It was an illusion, and in my opinion, it was snake oil.

Flush with success as a writer, he purchased a 600-acre Xanadu in the Catskills, where he planned to establish "the world's first university-sized Success School." Royalties dried up, takers for his syndicated success column dwindled. Hill was evicted, and the owner foreclosed on Xanadu.

In 1936, Napoleon Hill, barely scraping by at fifty-three years old, married a young and beautiful woman after she attended one of his lectures. She pestered him into writing *The Thirteen Steps to Riches*. Pelton agreed to publish it, but he wanted a catchy title, suggesting *Use Your Noodle to Win More Boodle*. They settled on *Think and Grow Rich*.

The wife went on to write a book called *How to Attract Men and Money*. Ironically, the book was released the year of their divorce, and she ended up with everything, including Hill's house and fancy cars.

W. Clement Stone, a self-made billionaire, and an avid fan of Hill's, one day purchased the rights to the book and presented them as a gift to the writer. As a result, Hill died a millionaire, but he had made and lost many fortunes during his lifetime, trying to find the laws of success for the ordinary man to obey and thus grow rich. His simple formula was the cultivation of faith, belief, persistence, patience, purpose, and desire, but it failed to work for Hill.

Napoleon Hill's life did not seem to me to be that different from either George's or Harry's. The three lives showed patterns of behavior that led to failure. In 1983, that was not what I wanted for my life. I wanted to be like a top chef rather than the food critic. I wanted to be like the tycoons who actually made a success of their lives, not the guy who watched from a distance full of admiration.

Many people claim that Hill's book has been of great help to them in their endeavors to succeed. I preferred, however, to take the advice of men and women who had actually succeeded at something.

I dove back into the biographies of self-made men and women. People like Henry Ford and Cornelius Vanderbilt had systems for idea generation. Vanderbilt's father was a ferryman, and Cornelius started out repeating the family pattern. He spoke of wanting to break away, and making a different mark in life. Mary Ellen Pleasant, who as a slave was sold three times to different owners, deliberately set about creating ideas that could help her break away from that life of slavery followed by servitude. She amassed a fortune equivalent to $600 million at today's value.

As inspired as I was by their stories, I was equally intrigued that their systems for creating ideas were so similar. This system is Step Two of *Three Simple Steps.* You will not find it in Hill's published book, although it's interesting that something similar was in the original manuscript.

Hill called his system the "Invisible Counselors Technique" and claimed that it allowed him to tap into the imaginary minds of anyone living or passed on, to source ideas and inspirations. Hill said, *"While the meetings of my cabinet may be purely fictional, and the meetings existent only in my own imagination, they have led me into glorious paths of adventure, rekindled an appreciation of true greatness, encouraged creative endeavor, and emboldened the expression of honest thought."*

Later, publishers edited out large parts of this chapter, fearing that Hill's devout Christian audience might question his sanity.

I have no such fear, because I do not need this book to make me rich. What you are about to read may at times seem unusual coming from a successful and pragmatic businessman, but it is what many successful self-made men and women claim made the difference between a life of adventure and a life in the quicksand. All it takes is one thought, one nanosecond of inspiration, to change your life forever, but you have to behave a little crazily to get it.

5

Creating Moments of Insight

I knew there was a way out; I knew there was another kind of life because I had read about it. I knew there were other places, and there was another way of being.

OPRAH WINFREY,
who having been raped, and abused, arrived on her father's doorsteps as a pregnant fourteen-year-old delinquent. Under his care, she was required to read and write a report on one inspirational library book a week.

IN 2007, HARVARD MEDICAL School conducted a study with volunteers in a lab, who were asked to learn and practice a five-finger piano exercise. A neuroscientist instructed the members of one group to play as fluidly as they could, trying to keep to the metronome's sixty beats per minute. Every day for five days, the volunteers practiced for two hours, and then underwent a transcranial-magnetic-stimulation test, which allowed scientists to infer the function of neurons.

The tests showed that after a week of practice, the stretch of motor cortex devoted to these finger movements took over surrounding areas. The finding was in line with a growing number of discoveries showing that greater use of a particular muscle causes the brain to devote more cortical growth to it.

Another group of volunteers were asked merely to think about practicing the piano exercise. They played the simple piece of music in their heads, holding their hands still while imagining how they would move their fingers. When scientists compared the test data on the two groups, they found the region of motor cortex that controls the piano-playing fingers also expanded in the brains of volunteers who imagined playing the music. The discovery showed that *mental training had the power to change the physical structure of the brain, and that the brain cannot distinguish between the physical and the imagined.*

In neuroscience, the prevailing belief was that the adult human brain is essentially hard-wired, so that by the time we reach adulthood we are pretty much stuck with what we have. Now, in its place, came the realization that the adult brain retains impressive powers of neuroplasticity—the ability to change its structure and function in response to experiences either real or *imagined.*

Until the 1980s, science believed the nervous system to be fixed and incapable of regeneration. Growth of neurons was considered most active during prenatal development. As we age, neurons atrophy. Now scientists believe new neurons are born continually throughout adulthood. Following a number of studies, such as the one described above, scientists even dare to suggest that we can rewire the brain.

Step Two is all about rewiring our neural networks such that it becomes natural for us to create brilliant ideas. There are three aspects to the second step. The first is recognizing patterns of unwanted behavior. The second is to consider the implications of changing those patterns, because change is not for everyone, and then committing to keep or change those patterns.

The third is a technique to change the way our brains work so that moments of insight become more common.

CHANGING PATTERNS OF BEHAVIOR

Just as I recognized the patterns of behavior in my ancestral line, you need to contemplate your own situation. Because your environment produces your mentality, you tend to adopt the same patterns of behavior as those you look up to. It is recognized that those who have been abused can more easily become abusers. People who endure a bad relationship tend to repeat the experience through life.

Professions such as physicians or lawyers often repeat through family lines, and I can trace the influence of soldiering in mine. That is not an issue, but along with the job, we often reproduce the attitudes, behaviors, and beliefs, some of which could be harmful to the pioneering spirit we need if we want to get out of quicksand. Take some time to review the lives of your ancestors. If you consider that they were stuck in quicksand, chances are you exhibit similar patterns in some aspects of your life.

A friend of mine split from her partner after thirteen years and much psychological abuse. In the last seven years, she has had four different relationships, each of which seemed to me like a clone of her first. Each one has ended abruptly when possessiveness became an issue. Our friend cannot see that she is attracting the same kind of partner and repeating the same behavioral pattern with each of her chosen mates.

Recently, I had dinner with this friend's mother, and learned of her three abusive relationships with the three different fathers my friend had grown up with. Mother and daughter repeated the pattern, just like George and Harry.

Another friend is continually moving from one job to another. After each move, she tells me how hard it was to work with a certain person who made her life miserable. Having worked with her, I am fairly sure that the cause of the problem is my friend, whose work style is paranoid and inflexible. She cannot see that she is repeating the pattern and triggering the repetitive response in a colleague.

Once we open our eyes and minds, we can see these behavioral patterns everywhere. Take a pleasant hour in a quiet place to consider what repeated emotions, thoughts, and reactions appear in your jobs, social networks, and relationships. Do you find yourself job-hopping? Are you in and out of debt? You are not to blame, and neither are your parents or partners. The patterns exist because your mentality has been unguarded and your neurons are wired a certain way. Now that you have control of your mentality, changes to behavior in those aspects of your life will result in changes to your neurons and catapult you forward. You do, however, have to want to change, and before you decide, you need to consider three major implications of change.

1. **Change can be imperceptible.**

Once you figure out what patterns you need to change in your life, those things won't always change in the direction you expect. When it comes to success mentality, I call the way things change *the way of the winding staircase.* Consider the desire to move from the ground floor to the second story. Because you are confident the stairs are connected to the second floor, you don't hesitate to take them. You have done it a thousand times and your neurons are wired such that you know when to start and when to stop.

Now imagine that a friendly Martian beams into the room, and asks to see your bedroom. You show her the stairs, and tell her to start climbing. Because she beams from one place to another, she has never seen stairs before and her neurons don't know what to do. At most parts of the winding staircase, she is facing away from the direction that she wants to go. Because she does not have certainty that the stairs are connected to her intended destination, the first time she turns a corner she thinks it a trick and descends.

In my life, achievement has often come the way of the winding staircase. It is all too easy to become discouraged when we can't see, and therefore believe, we are heading in the right direction. You have to trust in the way of the winding staircase because, when it comes to success, seeing is not believing, but believing leads to seeing. When you commit to change, it means staying on the staircase, no matter what. It is the unshakeable belief I discovered in every successful self-made person I read about, even Hill.

2. Change can be scary.

The techniques described in this book work completely. They don't work fractionally or within a range. If you have been thinking about debt you don't want and also dreaming about wealth in equal measures, what shows up in your life is the sum total of that equation, which is nothing, because they have cancelled each other out. This is an exact science. The thoughts you send out become your reality, not a diluted version of them.

Once you tip the balance in your favor by exercising more mentality control, things change dramatically. Your performance at work will improve, and you will get noticed. Promotion brings more responsibility. You may change jobs, perhaps careers, or you could move to new states or countries. In leaving the quicksand, you also often leave many of the people you have been with through your whole life to this point. Do you have the courage to walk away without looking back, knowing perhaps that there is resentment, envy, and criticism left behind?

If you are sure, then the next important step is to make a formal commitment to change. If you decided to trade in your car, you would expect to invest the time in researching the new choice. You might visit a dealership or two. You would sit down at someone's desk and negotiate pricing. Then you would formally commit to a purchase, which would include signing a document. When you go to that extent just for a lump of metal, why would you take committing to changing your life any less seriously?

3. Change is permanent.

There's a popular story in which a person sells his or her soul to the devil for personal gain, but then changes his or her mind and tries to cancel the covenant. Once made, however, a covenant cannot be broken. You are going to make a covenant with yourself, and because it cannot be withdrawn, you should treat the process with the same reverence as you would a job interview or car purchase.

The adventures you set in motion when you commit to change your life cannot be undone. There is no going back and no returning to the old friendships or your prior boss. This change is for real and it is permanent. Are you absolutely sure you want to change your life?

A COMMITMENT TO CHANGE

If so, then to get in the right mindset to make a commitment to change, I suggest you set this up as a formal appointment. Make it official so it achieves the right degree of importance in your life. Add it to a calendar as you would a business meeting. It might feel silly to make a formal appointment with yourself but compared to what I am going to ask you to do later, this is only mildly insane. Besides, no one needs to know about it but you.

By treating this formally, you ensure you do not fall into the trap of letting something in your life interrupt or overtake it. Nothing is more important than your personal growth. I treat all personal growth techniques and events with the same reverence and importance as any business meeting.

For the location, select a place that has special meaning for you. It should be a quiet place, and if possible, outdoors or connected to nature in some way. A park bench or riverbank is ideal.

I like to go to a particular beach cove whenever I need to make a commitment to a new direction. It is hard to access, but I am usually certain to be alone. I take a blanket and comfortable clothes. A glass of wine helps me relax, and I always take some of my favorite snacks. Doing this in a ritualistic style ensures I don't fall into the trap of rushing or skipping anything. Of course, I take a pad and pen. It is essential to do this alone. Above all, switch off that cell phone or pager.

For most people, this is a tougher task than it should be. The Center for Neural Decision Making at Temple University performed studies about how the brain processes information, which were reported in the *Denver Post* in 2011. Their research has found that as the flow of information increases, activity increases in the region of the brain responsible for decisions, solutions, and control of emotions but only up to a point. When the brain is flooded with too much information, activity in the same region suddenly drops off. The center for smart thinking shuts down at a time when you probably need it the most.

This has implications for the way we live our lives today. People admit to an almost compulsive need to answer emails, texts, tweets, and voice messages, and get nervous when their own do not receive immediate responses. The study showed that people find it impossible to take time off in our culture anymore without being anxious the whole time and with minds racing.

They concluded that "only when people take the time to quiet down the left brain, to forget about to-do lists and to un-plug from all input, solutions often percolate up from the sub-conscious. History is filled with stories like this. A period of not thinking about the problem, then the answer simply appears."

You are committing to change your life, so you have to shut off the outside world, and find a way to stop your mind racing just for a little while. Set up your place. Sit or lie comfortably. Uncork that wine. Shut off the phone. Shut down the left brain.

As you relax, gently review your situation in life without judg-ment or prejudice. Think about all the good things happening, the things you are grateful for, and the people you like. Consider some of the things you would change if you had a magic wand. What patterns of lifestyle or behavior have been trapping you? Imagine the joy of changing those.

Now try not to think about anything. To help with shutting down the left side of the brain, you can take your conscious self out of the way by simply focusing on your breath. Breathe deeply in and ex-hale forcefully. Follow the air as it enters your nostrils, sweeps down into your lungs, and forces your diaphragm down. As you exhale slowly, follow the warmed air back out of the lungs and down your nostrils, out into the universe. Pause for a moment and repeat. Repeat ten times, and if it helps, count each full breath.

This is a wonderfully relaxing exercise, and it has many health benefits. We are, however, only interested in one aspect, which is the way this allows you to access your neural network. It is not the mission of this book to explain why, but this simple breathing cycle is powerful. Please do not do the breathing cycle more than ten times.

One of the more exciting findings of contemporary brain research has been the brain's inherent plasticity. Neuroscientists have long seen that neurons and their dendrites—the physical structures behind thought and perception—act together to create brain patterns that we experience as thoughts and feelings. What they have now discovered is that this brain patterning is fluid and malleable. Even deeply embedded patterns can be changed through practices like cognitive shifting, and especially through distracting the conscious.

After a few minutes, or longer if you are enjoying the stillness, it is time to make your covenant. Take a pen and pad, and write down your decision.

I, (your full name), from this day forward, take full control of my mentality. I accept responsibility and accountability for my experiences. I intend abundance to flow in my life. I commit to change all patterns of destructive behavior, and to consistently introduce whatever it takes to succeed.

And then sign and date it.

If the thought of what change means scares you, it is equally important to make a covenant. Don't stay on the edge of quicksand but secretly wish you had changed or a life of frustration and disappointment is assured. Don't change but secretly wish you had stayed near the quicksand or a life of failures is guaranteed. Misery is caused by indecisiveness, so you must decide.

Then it is done, and your commitment is noted. Whether you know it or not, you are already among that fraction of people who are happier simply because they have made a decision. You are also out of the quicksand. Maybe someday you can help some others get out.

REWIRING THE MIND

If you have been practicing control of mentality, you will already be experiencing delightful changes in your life. Positive thinking is like a helium balloon, and negative thoughts are the ceiling they press against. Remove the ceiling by shutting out all that negative noise, and the balloon soars.

You notice changes in your environment. The sunshine really does seem brighter, the flowers more colorful. You may also notice the stars at night for the first time in ages. People with a cheerier disposition are attracted to you, so there is more laughter in your day. You get compliments out of nowhere and perhaps asked if it is a new hairstyle, clothes, or a diet. When people ask you how you are feeling, you tell them you are feeling great—because you are! You start to feel a buzz inside, the sort of buzz you have not felt since you were a very small child. It is the excitement of a great adventure ahead.

With some degree of control established, we can now work on rewiring your brain so that it can generate the brilliant ideas you need and that you probably thought were the province of only intellectuals and geniuses. The main method is a simple meditative technique that I call *Taking Quiet Time*. It requires no experience, no skill, and anyone from age five to eighty-five can start tomorrow and enjoy the same benefits in their ability to wire a new neural network that will be the source of critical moments of insight.

Taking Quiet Time

In the stories of self-made men and women, I was fascinated that most had some method of escaping the craziness of their schedules to sit quietly somewhere just to contemplate. They claimed their best ideas came to them when they stopped pondering the problem. They all had different ways of describing the process, depending on what was acceptable to believe at the time. The common elements for their systems of idea creation were contemplation time taken alone and, where possible, far from the madding crowd, daily practice, early in the day, and informal.

The human brain contains approximately a hundred billion neurons. It's possible your brain has more neural connections than there are stars in the universe! Neurons in your cerebellum can have one million connections each. The average person fires more neurons in a day than all the cell phone connections on the planet. Your brain is alive and ever changing with neurons disengaging and engaging in new neural networks constantly.

We develop neural networks two ways. When we learn something new, we utilize what we already know to understand better the thing we do not know. Our brain reaches for the familiar. Using the law of association, your brain fires new neural connections to create understanding.

The law of association is a law of psychology that is based on the teachings of Aristotle. Neurons that did not previously connect now do and a new neural network forms. If we do the same thing repeatedly, it becomes familiar, unconscious, and effortless. When you learn something new and repeat it in your mind, you are actually creating a neural network based on the law of repetition, another psychology law. When we build neural networks, a substance called Neural Growth Factor (NGF) actually "hard wires" the neurons together. Significantly, if an old neural network is not working properly, it may lose the NGF holding it together, and now we begin to see the benefit of mentality control.

In addition, *when we consciously change a neural network through hypnosis or another intervention such as meditation, we break down the existing NGF and rewire the network to new ways of thinking.* (*Rewire Your Brain; Think Your Way to a Better Life,* by John B. Arden, PhD)

Before we get into this simple technique, I need to address the fact that some of you may already practice yoga, tai chi, meditation, or some other discipline that aims at achieving spiritual and health improvement. Taking quiet time does not have those aims. It is purely a system of problem solving. Its aim is to find your path away from the quicksand. The benefit is the production of new neurons and neural pathways that, once they are protected from negativity and fear via mentality control, are the source of those wonderful, life-changing moments of insight. I am not suggesting you give up or change the other practices you enjoy. Taking quiet time is a separate, necessary step, and for many of you will be an additional activity in your day.

The taking quiet time technique has three parts to it. First is relaxation, second is finding stillness, and third is mental imagery. The whole thing takes about twenty minutes. It requires no skill or experience, and there are no advanced levels. The technique, or versions of it, can be found in most other spiritual and mental practices, but because those activities have a different intention the technique gets absorbed and produces a different result. Think of those practices, such as yoga, as a baked cake. In yoga or any other discipline, there are many ingredients, added in a certain order and baked a particular way to achieve a delicious, airy sponge. With taking quiet time, what we are doing is taking a couple of the same ingredients and using them differently to get a result that is as different in texture and taste as an omelet is to a cupcake.

Be careful not to confuse quietness with silence. Silence is hard to achieve. Sound is the brain's interpretation of the vibrating cilia in the ear in response to airwaves. Unless you remove all air from your environment and within your body, you cannot find silence. So don't try. Emotions are also a form of noise. By quietness, I mean a sense of calm or stillness. Stillness, like the still of the night, is a calm, motionless existence, devoid of thought or emotion. It is emptiness. It is close to nothingness, and the closer we get to that, the closer we get to all of our potential and the more ideas we will have.

In life, we get infrequent reminders of what this stillness feels like. It is that nanosecond of magic when a baby's hand closes around your extended finger or the sense of infinity as the sun slips below the horizon or knowing eyes briefly connect across a crowded room. We barely notice ourselves disappear in those times, but we do.

The insanity I prescribe is that taking quiet time needs to become a daily habit, and it requires you not to switch on the computer, radio, television, or cell phone first. It is contrary to how we have learned to behave in this time and place. Taking quiet time becomes the number one business growth tool in your arsenal, and the aim is to make it one of the first things you do every day. Here is the technique I recommend:

1. Alone

Taking quiet time must be a technique you practice alone. You might currently enjoy meditating with a friend, partner, or group, but with this second step you must be alone. We are aiming to return to the nothingness of the newborn individual, and that requires you to separate from the powerful energy of other people's thoughts and intentions. You would never think of having both radio and television volumes on at the same time in the same room. It would sound chaotic and probably irritating. With taking quiet times, thought energies would mingle and cause destructive interference. Solitude is essential.

2. Early in the day

Because our days are filled with sensory input right up until we fall asleep at night, this process is best undertaken early after waking. Where and when possible, it should be among the first things we do after waking. Quietness is only achievable while our minds are not yet fully awake, and we can tap into the inherent stillness of the dawn hours. To emphasize the importance of timing, we need to digress a moment to consider how men and women think differently.

Men tend to process thought in a linear way, taking one thing at a time. Our brains are like clipboards with a list of items and checkboxes. When we complete one task, we tick the box and move on to the next. Hence, taking quiet time first thing in the morning gives it the necessary priority and guarantees it gets done. Do it, check it off. Move on.

Women have the capacity to multitask mentally. All in the same moment, they can be thinking about what to wear, what to put in the kids' lunch boxes, how much milk is left in the fridge, how they should approach the issue of a raise with their boss, whether to ask the neighbors over for dinner on Friday night, what would be the best time and menu, and what did their husband really mean by that comment last night in bed. (I, of course, had completely forgotten I made the comment, and never meant anything by it in the first place, but that explanation will never make her thought go away.)

Therefore, if a woman tries to take quiet time at any time other than early in the morning, it will be harder for her to shut the left side of the brain down.

If you can find alone time and space where you live, then no matter what time you get up now, set the alarm clock to wake you thirty minutes earlier. If you live in a busy household, you should strive to be the first person up or else the distractions will destroy the process. Sounds are not so much an issue as the emotions they carry. Quietness requires emotionless contemplation.

Of course, reality is not so straightforward. There are other things we might do after waking, and this is not intended to be a military discipline. You may have valid reasons you can't get up half an hour before anyone else wakes or steal away to a private place. The imperatives are that you take quiet time alone and as early in the day as you can manage.

3. Silent, comfortable space

Choose as silent a place as you can find, one away from as many interrupting sounds as possible. There are always distracting sounds including internal ones, so don't stress about it. The hum of electricity is almost always in the air, and our stomachs might growl for breakfast. That does not matter. Wherever that place is for you, try to make it comfortable so you look forward to being there every morning. A comfy chair in a quiet corner, with a towel or blanket to keep you warm, is sufficient. Think minimalist here. A chair, a cushion, or a sofa in a corner of a room is fine. If you have a room with a window that looks out onto something natural like a tree, you are golden.

4. Sitting

Sit comfortably. Don't lie down because at that time in the morning, it is too easy to fall back to sleep. A little extra sleep cannot harm, but we are aiming to achieve something powerful here. It sounds like an oxymoron, but we need to focus on nothing. For that, we need to be awake enough to control our thoughts. It doesn't matter how you position your legs so long as you are comfortable. It is what we do with our mind that counts, so all we aim for with the body is to get it relaxed and comfortable so it does not interrupt us for the next twenty minutes with aches and pains. I like to place my hands touching together in my lap. Feet can be apart but resting in contact with the floor. It is simply a re-laxed sitting position.

5. Energy cleansing

It can help if you clear the energy around you before you start. If you had unpleasant dreams or feel weary, rub the palms of your hands vigorously together until you can feel the heat energy being exchanged between them. Place a palm on each side of your forehead and drag your hands down your cheeks. Shake your hands as if air-drying them. Do this three times. Repeat for the crown of your head three times. Then cross your arms and brush your hands over the opposite shoulders and upper arms.

This technique seems a little "out there," doesn't it? Have you ever noticed, however, stressed workers or en-trepreneurs sitting at their desks, overwhelmed by a challenge? Don't they, at some point, put their heads in their hands? Have you ever seen them then brush their hands through their hair and sigh out loud, and then rest their interlocked fingers at the back of their necks?

The next time you watch something scary, like a horror movie, perhaps you might also notice that most people hide their eyes behind their hands, and then drag their fingers down their faces when the scary moment passes. It is a form of stress-energy clearing. We do it without thinking and also without knowing why we do it. It is ancient medicine, hardwired into our subconscious. There is nothing "new age" about it at all. The more detailed suggestion I have here was actually a common Native American practice performed by all members of a tribe before starting a meeting or ritual. When no one is looking, I do this several times a day and always find it refreshing. All we are doing is wiping away stale energy. It feels like wiping away the tiredness from our eyes, and it is rejuvenating.

6. Relaxation

Your eyes can be open or closed, but I find closed easier for concentration. Take a deep breath. As you exhale, do so with a sigh. Making a sound here helps concentration, and it feels good. Repeat a few times until you feel nicely relaxed. Now, sit as still as you can. Breathe normally, and let your mind become aware of your body in the chair. Take your concentration to your feet, legs, torso, head, and arms like a probe. Tell each part of your body to relax. Imagine your face and head, your spine, your heart, and your stomach relaxing. You start to feel as limp as a rag doll. It is a good feeling. Keep the quietness.

7. Connect with the ground

Once you feel more relaxed, it helps to imagine yourself connected to the Earth. This is another Native American technique that allows your mind to be more fully in the present. It reduces some of the chatter in your head. Simply spend a few seconds taking your awareness down to your feet. Imagine roots growing from the soles of your feet and down through the floor, through the walls, into the foundation, down into the soil, and farther down toward the Earth's core. Don't spend too much time trying to get the image perfect. Just a few seconds of imagining those roots connecting with the Earth has a very useful grounding benefit.

8. Follow the breath

When you feel relaxed, it is time to distract your left brain. The goal is to think of nothing. This is unnatural. Focus on your normal breathing—in and out. Just as you did when committing to change, follow it with your imagination as it goes in through the nose, curling into the lungs, and back out. Keep stillness. Try to do nothing but follow the breathing. Counting in and out is fine. This time, we are not going for deep breaths. Breathe normally. Follow the air with your concentration. Do this for around ten to twenty minutes. You don't need to keep formal time. Your mind will tell you when it has recharged sufficiently. If you are like most people, you follow your breath a few times, and then suddenly realize that your mind has drifted back to some everyday thought. Don't fret. That is your ego, indignant about being set aside. It happens to everyone. Just smile and refocus on your breath. Get stillness back. Taking quiet time works in ways we don't need to understand, so just enjoy this wonderful personal time.

9. Stretch

Open your eyes. Smile. Stretch. Thank yourself for this gift of a few minutes peace. You deserve it. You just took 2 percent of your day for *you*. Do it every day. In Step Three, we will add an image exercise to do immediately after stretching. For now, just enjoy the benefit of taking quiet time.

When you take quiet time every day, you may not even realize that you achieved a few moments of stillness. Because it is nothingness, it is impossible for a human to notice. They can be nanoseconds in duration. Rest assured that many times during the exercise you regressed to nothingness, and new neural networks were fired up.

This rewiring of the brain is vital. The new networks have none of the old learned patterns of behavior. You are free to decide how to live for yourself. You are relearning how to be an individual again. They have none of the damage caused by negative impressions from media or people, so they have unlimited potential so long as you use mentality control to keep them that way.

In the weeks, months, and years ahead, you will build such a large reservoir of this nothingness that the rewiring builds its own momentum. Nanoseconds may even grow to seconds, and you will wonder where you just disappeared to. Keep in mind that the aim is not to stop thinking for twenty minutes. Only mystics can achieve that. Attempt to take quiet time daily, nothing more.

My best ideas come when meditating.

DANIEL LOEB,
a teenage surfer turned investor and now worth
more than $4 billion

In 2007, a study conducted at UCLA was reported in *ScienceDaily* that provided the first neural evidence of why "mindfulness," which they described as the "ability to live in the present moment, without distraction" seems to produce a variety of health benefits. Although this book is not concerned with that particular benefit of taking quiet time, the study drew interesting conclusions.

The technique they used was very similar to the one described in my "Taking Quiet Time" approach and with a focus on following the breath. Participants followed their breathing without judgment, released their thoughts, and "just let go." Then Functional Magnetic Resonance Imaging was used to study the subjects' brain activity when they were shown pictures of common expressions and asked to give them an emotional label.

They found that the more participants let go, the more activation was seen in the right ventrolateral prefrontal cortex, and the less activation in the amygdala. They also saw activation in widespread centers of the prefrontal cortex. Their "so what" for this is that it demonstrated an activation pattern similar to the effects of dampening chronic pain and raising mood.

They concluded, "This is such an exciting study because it brings together the Buddha teachings, more than 2,500 years ago with modern neuroscience . . . now for the first time since those teachings, we have shown there is actually a neurological reason for doing mindfulness meditation. Our findings are consistent with what mindfulness meditation teachers have taught for thousands of years."

A Personal History of Taking Quiet Time

I had read many biographies in which the subject found a way to escape the madding crowd by practicing some form of contemplation or meditation. I knew I had to try it and was motivated to change the pattern of learned behavior that I recognized in my ancestors. In those biographies, people claimed their time of solitude was the source of moments of insight. If it worked for them, I figured who was I to think it esoteric nonsense?

I worked shifts at a busy teaching hospital, so with the aid of two alarm clocks, one on the bedside table and one under my pillow, I literally had to force myself to get up an extra half hour early, bump from wall to wall through the darkened house so as not to disturb my wife or dog, and find my way to a quiet corner in the back bedroom.

In those days, cash was tight, and the heat did not turn on until the evening. Wrapping myself in clothes and blankets, I sat upright in a wooden chair, and stared out through the window at the streetlights, which were usually distorted by rain.

My mind was always full of chatter, which I found frustrating at first, and sometimes I was so dog-tired from the previous shift, I fell asleep again. I was easily interrupted by outside noises— the electric whine of the milk van and clink of the milkman's bottles as he made deliveries to every house in the street. The chorus of dawn birds and the early commuter traffic would draw my attention. I used to feel that my ears deliberately tuned in to the noises and amplified them, just to drive me nuts.

Our small, three-room house overlooked the main road, and the thin windows offered little protection from sound or cold. The secret is just to stick with it long enough for it to become a habit. Eventually, the noises ceased being disturbing, and the mind learns to set itself aside. Once it becomes habit, it becomes natural and easy. But you have to stick it out long enough to achieve that.

At the outset, I didn't understand that the goal was stillness rather than silence, and that was probably the cause of my frustration. With practice, however, I made the external noises part of the process. I stopped being *against* them, and then they no longer bothered me. Today, I actually miss the sound of those clanking milk bottles.

There is no getting away from it—taking quiet time in the morning takes discipline. Anyone can do it for a few days in a row, but then your ego tries to turn you back to the old habits, and you have to fight for the new habit. I don't know how long you have to stick at it before you make it a habit. It is probably different for everyone. I remember feeling it was quite a chore for a long time, perhaps weeks. Today, however, it is one of the things I look forward to the most every day.

Early on, I made the mistake of telling people what I was doing and received ridicule in return. This is something best kept to yourself. Why invite negative energy into your mentality when you don't have to? The teasing made me question my sanity. My wife, however, encouraged me to stick it out because she could see real benefits, both in my demeanor and in the miracles that started happening in our life.

Within a few weeks, I noticed marked changes in my ability to solve puzzles and challenges. While I was sitting in a meeting room while my peers wrestled with an issue, an insight would pop into my head. Where it came from I could not say, but often I left the people in the room stunned by the clarity of the solution. I was equally stunned, but smart enough not to admit it. Over the years, I heard other people describe these moments of insight as *brilliant* or *uncanny,* and I developed a reputation as something of a troubleshooter. I found myself being sought after to join other teams' projects.

Once we close our eyes, we could be anywhere, so the location is not as important as the doing of it. When traveling I have contented myself with sitting on a hotel room floor with my back to a wall. Later, as miracles started to show up in my life, my Taking Quiet Time place changed. I had the luxury of a comfortable couch in a warm sunroom, then a tower room overlooking the ocean.

Today, I walk barefoot across a warm patio, surrounded by beautiful landscaping where a gentle waterfall runs into a pond. Hummingbirds feed from red hibiscus flowers around a raised terrace overlooking a seemingly endless view. I sit in the shade of the wisteria and listen for a while to the myriad of birds chirping in our private garden before closing my eyes and disappearing for twenty minutes.

Everything about my quiet time setting has changed for the better, and I mention it this way so you know what you also have to look forward to. It matters not where or how you start but where and how you end up. When I close my eyes, however, I could just as easily be in a hotel room. The location is unimportant. It takes less than two percent of our day. As busy creators, don't we deserve that much time to ourselves when the benefit is so great from something so easily practiced?

In the beginning, I was fortunate to be able to get up early and find alone time most days. I think that helped me establish a good habit. Over time, I have had to mix things up, although I always found a way to fit it in before heading off to work. Sometimes I had to wait until everyone left the house to sneak upstairs for twenty minutes of quiet time and breathing before heading off to work myself. Other times, the only alone space I could find was in my car, and I would take twenty minutes or so before heading out of the garage. It was not ideal, but I'm a believer in "every little bit helps."

These days, my wife and I typically take turns getting up first. The first one up makes a pot of tea, and the second one up gets the luxury of an extra fifteen minutes in bed. I take my tea outdoors to enjoy the view. When I've drunk my tea, I take my quiet time, which never lasts more than twenty minutes. It is as important to me today as it was in 1983, and I could not imagine my life without it.

My advice is to be as disciplined in the beginning as your situation and lifestyle allow. Just find a way to get it into your schedule. If you close your eyes and follow your breath while traveling on a packed subway, you will still get a benefit, and perhaps someday enough of those benefits will get you out of the quicksand of the sardine commute. Don't let any situation be an excuse to avoid taking quiet time altogether.

The question now is what to do with our newly rewired neural networks. Like any wires, they are simply potential until we plug them into an energy source. Before you knew how to control your mentality, you might simply have wired them back into the chronic complainers or sensational news headlines. To get those great ideas we are looking for, however, we need to plug the network into a powerful and beneficial source.

PLUGGING IN

The evening was cool and crisp, with a light easterly breeze. Tree limbs moved lazily with the wind, swaying with a hypnotic, almost spiritual motion that brought peace of heart and mind to those in tune with nature. The moon had risen high in the sky and was perched behind a thick, gray rain cloud that changed shapes as it gradually made its way across the evening sky. The moonbeams, the clouds, and the wind all worked together to create dancing shadows that leaped and flickered across the valley below. The gentle chirping of crickets, and songs of the cicadas were the only sounds that broke the silence at Paha Sapa. It was at times like these that you knew why these hills were sacred, and were called the heart of everything that is.

David and the Man sat beneath the giant oak where David had learned the secret of happiness. The Man chanted softly, and his tone mixed with the sounds of nature in perfect harmony. They had not spoken for many hours. Together they had watched the sun sink below the horizon and had greeted the night with silence. In his heart, David felt peace. He looked to the stars and saw their mystery; he felt the strength of the wind on his face and heard Wakantanka in the creatures of the night. He was awed by this place, yet he felt as if he belonged here.

Finally, as the evening drew on, David spoke. "I have a question."

"Yes?"

"I was wondering how much everything has changed since you were a young boy."

The Man sighed and looked at the ground. He seemed almost saddened by his answer. "They have changed very much."

"How?"

"In many ways."

"Tell me, what were our people like many years ago?"

The Man thought for a long while. "We were much closer to Mother Earth in the past. Our ways have been slowly forgotten or neglected. There are too many who feel they do not have a place in the world of today."

In his heart, David knew the words were true. People do not feel a kinship with the world. What was it his father said? A man's heart becomes hard when it's taken from nature. It changes him forever. It creates a lack of respect for the earth and all growing, living things, and in the end, leads to a lack of respect for humans, too.

David felt sorrow for the Man. The world could still learn from him, but would the world ever give him the chance? It should. In the ever-changing world of today, the Man's teachings could bring stability and peace of heart to all those in need.

—Excerpt from *Lessons of a Lakota: A Young Man's Journey to Happiness and Self-Understanding* by Billy Mills with Nicholas Sparks

Another character trait that jumped out at me from the pages of the biographies of self-made men and women was their affiliations with nature. All of them turned to nature in times of stress or when big decisions needed to be made.

Henry Ford was passionate about walking in the country and reconnecting to nature. He encouraged workers to exercise in their off-hours and believed that next to work, it was a man's duty to think. For his thinking time, he retreated to an old farmhouse near the Ford dairy in Dearborn. He sat on the ground when it was dry and in an old rocking chair when it was wet and simply let thoughts come to him. He shared his philosophy with Ralph Waldo Trine in a 1920s book titled *Power That Wins*. He offered this dictum: "Let every man think for himself. Let him call a conference for his powers, his common sense in the chair, his desire and knowledge of things as they are pleading the case before him."

Emerson was another who attributed his success, and his sense of tranquility through it, to being at one with nature. He spent as much time walking in a forest as working in an office because that is where he found his inspiration.

. . . of Nature itself upon the soul; the sunrise, the haze of autumn, the winter starlight seem interlocutors; the prevailing sense is that of an exposition in poetry; a high discourse, the voice of the speaker seems to breathe as much from the landscape as from his own breast; it is Nature communing with the seer.

RALPH WALDO EMERSON

To channel his restlessness, Cornelius Vanderbilt's mother paid him to clear and plant an eight-acre field. In that solitude, he came up with the ideas that made him a billionaire. John Jacob Astor, son of a German butcher, arrived in New York as a penniless immigrant. He became enchanted by the American wilderness and, within a year, was up the Hudson River making a living in the fur trade. In his biography, it is claimed that he imagined his future while daydreaming in the cool shadows of American oaks.

Harry's craving for cigarettes was one of the things that changed my life because it forced me outdoors. I would arrive home from school and realize he had spent most of the day sitting in a closed room while smoking cigarettes and reading. The farmhouse had its original seventeenth-century walls, which retained generations of dampness. The only source of heat was a solitary coal fire in the hearth. It spewed gaseous fumes in all directions. My father smoked forty cigarettes a day, and the small room trapped a thick, blue, noxious haze. Above his armchair, yellow nicotine patches stained the ceiling.

It was like blowing smoke into an inflated balloon, and when I opened the door, a cloud of gas and smoke enveloped me. It did me no good to complain, so at every opportunity, I would escape that environment and head outdoors. The countryside air was like nectar by comparison. The nearest neighbor was a mile south, and I could walk north for five miles without seeing another person or breathing in anything but fresh air. To have such space at that age was liberating.

When it was warm, I walked barefoot across the fields. When it rained, I stood in streams to feel the gathering pace of the runoff. I walked in the woods and listened to all the sounds of falling leaves, dripping rain, and scurrying feet in the undergrowth. I began to understand how connected everything in the forest was. At first I felt like an intruder, but over time the noise ceased to be individual sounds and became a symphony, and the animals gradually accepted my presence. I learned to walk stealthily, downwind of where wild animals foraged. I could stand still as a tree trunk and watch them for hours without them fearing me.

My siblings thought I had turned nerdy. Because I did not watch television in the domestic fog with them, my parents worried that I was becoming a loner. I simply preferred being outdoors to the choking environment of the lounge. There was no more intention behind it than that.

When I stayed out all evening, in rain or clear skies, everyone suspected that I was up to no good or had a secret girlfriend in the village. I was up to nothing more, however, than getting away from the pollution of the village house and street lamps, so as to take in the starry sky.

Odd things started to happen to me, things that I never mentioned to anyone at the time for fear of ridicule. I started to develop what I would call back then an extra-sensory perception. Today, I know it simply as my normal senses awakening through their reconnection with the unifying energy of nature, an experience available to everyone. Like the animals, I sensed a thunderstorm coming even when the sky was cloudless. I became aware of people's presence before they stepped into a room. I knew when people were thinking or talking about me. I could physically feel it in my solar plexus and still do today.

My levels of concentration at school improved, and I played a higher level of sports. At school and at home, I would often offer an answer or comment to something that had not yet been spoken. "How did you know what I was thinking?" was a question I was commonly asked.

When circumstances kept me indoors, such as a day of torrential rain or a need to stay in to do homework, I noticed how my senses diminished, even after a day or two. My schoolwork deteriorated because I felt lethargic and sleepy in class. I performed less well on the soccer team. Within a few hours of returning to nature, I felt refreshed. It became like a drug to me.

As I read more biographies, I noted the emphasis successful people placed on connecting to nature. George Washington Carver was a famous American scientist, educator, and inventor, best known for changing the direction of the American agricultural industry. He was born into slavery and all eleven of his siblings died at young ages. When slavery was abolished, black people were not allowed to go to the public schools. These barriers did not prevent Carver from educating himself. He went on to be an advisor to three American presidents and to promote racial harmony. His quote best describes the benefit of rewiring our network into nature at every opportunity: *I love to think of nature as an unlimited broadcasting station, through which God speaks to us every hour, if we only will tune in.*

Another benefit of being alone in open spaces when I was younger was that I could talk out loud, and no one would hear. When little children act out imaginary games, onlookers smile. When a teenager does it, parents send them to a psychologist. Adults get locked away. Imagination, however, is a key attribute for success. Everything I have achieved in my life was first played out in my mind's eye, many of them during those early days of make-believe in the countryside.

North of the farmhouse, the landscape rose gently for several miles. The views from the brow of the hill extended in all directions and as far as the eye could see. Like a living scarecrow, a gnarled rowan tree stood in the center of a five-acre field. I spent hundreds of hours sitting under the protection of its branches, simply watching the view or reading an inspiring book.

Since then, I have always taken steps to stay energized by nature. I have lived in cities, apartment blocks, and suburbia, where nature's presence is not as obvious. It is, however, still possible to connect with her in simple ways, by walking around the block, sitting in a park, or walking along a canal. I think of it as a matrix into which we plug our neural networks. That gives us the opportunity to connect with a larger store of knowledge.

There are various modern definitions of the matrix, none of which satisfy the complexity of the subtle energy connections taking place when we commune with nature. Hollywood portrays it as humans electrifying an external reality run by dominant machines, which is not just incorrect but flat out backwards.

Early civilizations referred to Mother Earth as a matrix. They perceived people, animals, the earth, and the universe as unified, and achieved a symbiotic interconnection. That is the genuine matrix, and we need to plug our new neurons into it. We were, indeed, much closer to Mother Earth once, and making small, subtle attempts to get closer to her will enhance the benefits of Taking Quiet Time, because by plugging into nature's matrix, your brain can access an expanded reservoir of knowledge just as a single computer can plug into the World Wide Web.

Connection

After taking quiet time for a while (I can't say how long, as everyone is different), we find our perspective of the world shifts. As well as experiencing mental moments of brilliance, we feel less distant from others who were originally outside our environment of like-minded people. I find it hard to describe, but at the same time we feel more connected, while also feeling more individual. The picture I imagine is the connectedness a drop of rainwater, existing as an isolated system, still feels as part of the ocean from whence it came.

Our natural urge to criticize starts to diminish, and arguing seems like a waste of energy. What used to irritate us no longer feels as bothersome, and our emotions become more balanced.

People from our past might make contact again. There is an increase of what we currently regard as coincidences showing up in our lives. We could keep bumping into the same stranger in different places and yet not know why. We might be thinking of someone just before they call. Even if this already happens, we can be surprised how the incidences increase.

We then get urges to escape the urban concrete, and crave a walk in the country or a day at the beach. We want more plants in the office or to take greater care in the garden. These are signs of our new neurons seeking reconnection and that our subconscious is working with us to get plugged back into nature's matrix. We ignore it at our peril.

If you have not been controlling your mentality before you start taking quiet time, your neurons will still seek reconnection. The danger, however, is that they will grab onto the fear and anxiety that media and people around you donate. This is why it is critical to use the three steps in the order written in this book.

Imagine you just took your first period of taking quiet time but are ignoring the importance of mentality control. It might not have been a complete success, but boy you felt good having a half hour to yourself. For a while there you actually stopped thinking. You don't know why, but you felt energized after. Hope surged through you, and you went down to the kitchen with a spring in your step.

If you had been controlling your mentality, you might have chosen to put on an invisible mentality shield before the partner and kids descend. On this occasion, however, your mentality is still wide open. Chaos descends with the routine of a typical day. Your partner complains that you have not yet let the dog outside. In its excitement, the dog knocks a carton of milk off the table with its tail. Your child finds it funny, and your partner snaps at the child. Your thoughts are critical of the way your partner handled the situation, and you make a note to speak to him or her later about it.

When you finally leave for work, you switch on the car radio, which is always tuned to your preferred news program, and it blurts out that the stock market plummeted in early trading due to concerns about an economic crash in Eastern Europe and heightened tensions in the Middle East. An image of your diminishing pension plan flashes in your head, and your stomach turns as you briefly question how you will ever afford college funds for the kids.

Right now, all those new neurons have been wired right back into the old mentality. The situation and the thought cause you to react. You drive off a little aggressively. A passing car blares its horn at you, and you react further by giving the finger only to realize it was a neighbor—the one who you always have words with over one thing or another. By now, and in less time than you spent taking it, the quiet time seems like a distant memory. Its benefits have gone.

What you could have done was simply to lower that mentality shield around yourself before you left your quiet place. You might have answered your partner's jibe about the dog by simply smiling and taking the dog outside. Suddenly, you are connecting with nature. It does not matter where you are, there will be trees, grass, sky, birds, and fresh air. You will not even be aware of it, but your neurons will follow your attention. If you look at the sky and admire its color or the clouds or the wonderful feeling of raindrops on your skin, your neurons connect. If you smell a rose or touch a leaf, you immediately connect, however briefly, with nature. Through nature, you connect with everyone and everything.

When you get in the car, your radio is off because that day you decide you will take notice of the world around you instead of listening to all that doom and gloom. Your day is off to a better start, and because your neurons are wiring in a different pattern, who knows what miracles and adventures are in store?

When we connect to nature's matrix, it speeds up our rewiring, because we draw more energy through each new connection. Nature is electrified. Your physical and subtle bodies are an invigorated pattern of electromagnetic waves. When you reach out to touch something, whether a lover, a tree, or a blade of grass, a connection takes place, and vitality is exchanged.

Although most people cannot see or feel it, mini-explosions, like sparks, dance between them and anything they touch with one of their senses, and it works whether it is hearing, sight, smell, or touch.

Just as the quickest way to learn a new language is to move to a country where the populace speaks it, the best way to connect with the matrix is through immersion in nature.

Observing nature from a distance, such as through the window of a high-rise building, is like watching a bath being filled with water. It is no more than a vessel collecting fluid, but when you eventually immerse yourself in the warm, scented water, you get that wonderful *ahh* moment. Now you get it, the purpose of the bath. It is the same with nature. You have to be in it to get it.

Nature is a unified network. When you step into it often enough, you become part of it. Connected, you have access to the infinite source of nothingness, which, therefore, gives you unlimited potential to attract anything you want, including great ideas.

In business, we seem to have an inherent desire to disconnect from nature. We spend hours trapped in a box-like room that is made of dense materials and lit by artificial means. The ornamental plants are made of silk. Water is served up in plastic bottles. The view, if we have one, is hidden behind closed blinds. We turn our backs to Mother Earth, focusing not on gaining energy but in exchanging energy with the people around the table. It is hardly an environment conducive to fermenting ideas.

Small changes can make a big difference. Open a window. Let the sun in. Rearrange the furniture so people can see outside. Bring in some natural plants. Take frequent nature breaks, and encourage everyone to take their coffee outside for ten minutes. If you are running a meeting, I guarantee you will get better solutions and have a happier team.

With particularly difficult business decisions to face, I recommend breaking the traditional meeting room format. In 1997, I joined a start-up company that was staffed mainly by scientists. The company had little cash on hand, a high cash-burn rate, and no concept of direction. The new CEO, Bob, recognized that the company's prior management had accepted every research project that had come along. In effect, they had fourteen projects at a similar level of development, and none anywhere near to generating revenue. It was a juggernaut rolling steadily down a hill to the edge of a cliff.

Bob invited me to discuss the situation with him, and I was delighted to learn that the meeting was not going to be in a gloomy indoor environment but on his yacht. My previous company boasted a corporate, floating gin-palace, but I was never high enough up the food chain to be invited on a trip. With this opportunity to join Bob on his yacht, my ego went into overdrive, and I felt I had finally arrived. It was somewhat disappointing to discover that the yacht was a ten-foot dinghy, and because of my Navy background, he expected me to be an expert sailor.

At least I did not run us aground, and the few hours spent casually sailing in a light breeze proved to be critical to the company's survival. There is just something about being closer to nature that ignites those neurons. The company vice president joined us, and between us, we talked Bob into accepting that ten of the projects had to be stopped or sold off. We had four that stood a chance of making it, within the available budget, to start generating revenues and save the company.

We drew up a new company structure that could achieve the goal, be more cost-effective, and meet shareholder expectations. It was a unique approach to developing products in that industry. What makes it particularly impressive is that no one in the yacht had a scientific background. Bob came from the banking world. The vice president had been a nurse once, and grew into her role without business qualifications. I was a business development guy. I have no doubt that if we had tried to hold that meeting in a traditional office environment, the company would have been doomed.

In 2002, I faced a similar dilemma with a company that had three projects at similar stages of development. The senior executive team spent hours in the confines of a windowless boardroom, wrestling with the puzzle of moving these projects forward within a limited budget. The three scientists who ran each project had sizeable egos and spent much of the time talking over each other.

As an invited consultant, I convinced the team to take a break and walk with me around the block. The company lawyer thought I was just a nutty consultant and tried to escape back to his office to answer emails. I literally had to manhandle him out of the door.

Outside, I deliberately did not keep the business conversation going because I wanted the serenity of outdoors to rebalance the egos and reenergize the neurons. This sounds very new age when I write it, but it worked, so I just go with it now. I noticed how the posture of the three scientists changed as we walked. They became more upright. Their expressions opened up. It was like watching heavy weights fall off their shoulders. The tension left the team, and someone said something that made everyone laugh.

As we turned to head back to the office, the human resources manager, who had not uttered a word in the meeting room and appeared overawed by the scientific jargon flying about, spoke up. In an apologetic tone, he asked what was wrong with stopping two projects and putting all the eggs in one basket. At least, he said, they would stand one chance of making it as a company. I expected the three scientists to jump down his throat, but to my surprise there was a period of complete silence. Astoundingly, the scientist who had defended his project the loudest back in the boardroom now admitted that his team was losing faith in their ability to resolve certain challenges. He turned to a colleague and suggested that if he added his team and resources to one of the other projects, the combined team would stand a chance.

Back in the meeting room, the team drew up a new business plan to present to the board, and called it the "Texas Hold-'Em, All In plan." A week later, the board approved the idea. I received a lot of praise for getting this result from three scientists notorious for being difficult to work with. I did not do anything, however, except take the team outside for some fresh air. I understood very little about the science. In business, I find the solution to most problems already resides in the minds of the people struggling to find an answer. The secret is simply helping them to let it out.

Smell the Roses

For most people, life is pretty chaotic, and there just are not enough hours in the day. Life in the quicksand can feel that way because so much energy and time goes into the struggle to stay afloat. On top of that, now I am asking you to get up half an hour earlier and dedicate time to yourself.

There can be no compromise in taking quiet time. You made a covenant, a solemn promise to yourself, to change, and this is the way to do it. It is the only way I know to regenerate neurons. I am also going to encourage you to change routines and dedicate time to get back with nature. These are just small changes in lifestyle that will make a big difference to your life.

When your life is busy, you have to find a way to change schedules. The time you spend in the office taking a coffee break could be spent going outside for fresh air. Notice the clouds. Touch a tree. Smell a flower. Hear the birds. Each sense is a reconnection. Take your lunch to a park or sit near a body of water. No one but you needs to know what you are doing or why you no longer hang about at the coffee machine to gossip.

A child feels more connected to the planet than an adult. Walking barefoot on grass or playing with their hands in the dirt is as normal as eating and sleeping. You don't have to jump in puddles, but maybe you can walk part of the way to work instead of taking the bus every day.

Take a break from television and go outside to watch a starry sky. Five minutes is all it takes, and you will probably only miss a commercial break anyway. When was the last time you climbed a steep hill to take in the view? Now and again, take your shoes and socks off and walk on the grass. There are some people who believe doing the latter can cure any illness. All I know is it connects you a little more to nature and feels really good. Who doesn't get that giddy, child-like feeling when they see their bare toes in the grass?

When you touch the walls of your office, there is not much to connect with. Being of dense materials, they emit lower energy. With you vibrating at a higher frequency, you give more to the wall than it can give to you. There are many reasons why people who spend all day and night indoors become listless, weak, or ill, and this is one of them. They give their energy away without finding a way to restore it.

When you touch a tree, however, you fire off connections like an army of archers storming a castle. Because the tree is connected to the Earth through its roots, all of nature fires back. Your rewired neurons use nature's network in the same way the tree uses its roots.

Once a week, you would benefit from immersing yourself in nature for an hour or so. That means dedicating some time to really reconnect with nature, not just the glimpses and glances I've been encouraging up to this point. Go to a beach or a national park, and spend time just walking or sitting on a wall to take in a view. Perhaps one evening you can take your family for a walk together after dinner. I know that in our hectic lives it sometimes seems impossible, but these are not options. If you want to achieve success and a greater quality of life, it is essential to take the time and make some effort. For me, watching a sunset with my wife and dogs creates the same quality of stillness as holding a baby or taking quiet time.

When I was in my midtwenties and chose to take control of my destiny, many family members warned me that the higher up the food chain we go, the harder work it is. People at the top, they told me, have to work 24/7. I can tell you that the higher up the food chain I went, the more I used my brain over my body, and the more time I had to reconnect with nature. I also enjoyed my work so much that it ceased to feel like work at all.

Once again, I remind you that we are not trying to become masters. Simple, subtle changes to routine are all that are required to succeed. Change a little, change a lot. None of this is painful or expensive. Rather, everything I am suggesting is free, fun, and energizing.

6

Moments of Insight

IT TOOK ME A while to pluck up the courage to ask my future wife on a date. I thought she was engaged to someone, and she thought I was with someone else. The hospital staff knew differently and conjured up every trick they could to throw us together.

They finally succeeded; on our first date we did nothing more exciting than go for a late afternoon walk by the shore. When it was dark, we sat in a pub nursing one drink each until the landlord forced us out. We just never stopped talking and have not stopped since.

While she worked on the in-patient wards, I worked in the radiotherapy department in the same teaching hospital. The patients often lived far away and would stay in the hospital for several weeks while undergoing treatment for cancer. It was a rewarding experience to be part of their lives during those times.

I worked in a predominantly female department. Cliques had developed, and the environment away from the patients was one of toxic gossip. I wore my mentality shield all the time and separated myself from the background politics. It did not make me a popular workmate, but I was able to focus on what was important, which was the patients' welfare.

The department head had been in the job for more than thirty years and felt threatened by the fast pace of technological change. She gave promotions to anyone who swore their fealty, and I was certainly not considered a supporter. New ideas to improve effectiveness or patient experience were not welcomed, which was an issue for me, because I had new ones every day as a result of taking quiet time.

By 1987, I was tearing my hair out, and I felt I had to move on. During the previous twelve months, a few pharmaceutical companies contacted me about switching to a career in pharmaceutical sales. I turned them all down simply because I had allowed my mentality to form a negative image of what it meant to be a salesperson.

George and Harry had been salesmen off and on. When Harry ran the tire depot, I took my vehicle in for one replacement tire. One of his partners inspected the car and assured me I needed four new tires instead. Having no clue myself, I went along with it. After the job was completed, and I had paid in cash, I overheard him joking with my father that he just talked some sucker into buying four new tires he didn't need. My father looked outside to see who the sucker was. When he saw me, he slunk back to the safety of his desk without another word. That was his style. Whatever he could get away with was a triumph to him, no matter who was the victim. I also bought auto insurance from him only to discover after a traffic accident years later, and a subsequent court summons, that he used my cash for other things.

He sold mortgages to people who really could not afford them. He was only interested in making commissions and did not care what happened to his customers after that. Having never had a mortgage himself, he lied to them about his experience and most fell for it. Those observations had my neurons wired with a negative impression of the character required to be in sales.

At the same time, my wife was feeling a bit burned out after twelve years working on a cancer ward. She needed a break and, at the very least, a vacation, but our combined salaries barely covered the mortgage, and we had too much debt. Finances were tight and we lived on convenience food of the "just add water" variety. We were in financial quicksand. One of my dreams was to travel and experience other cultures and companies, and somehow that was not happening. I needed a rethink.

After taking quiet time one day, I somehow decided that I would take the next sales job offer that came along, and do it for only a couple of years until we recovered financially. That seemed like a good idea, and a compromise that could get me over my hang-up about salespeople. That might not sound like a moment of brilliance, but at the time it felt like it. If I could survive the military, I figured I could be a salesman for a couple of years. We would get back on our feet and also have some money for a vacation or two.

Not having a vehicle at that time, I cycled to one of my favorite scenic spots, a pond in the center of a village green. Once there, I went through a *commitment to change* ritual, exactly as outlined in this Step Two. Whenever a good idea comes to me, I do this exercise and write out a new statement that fixes the new idea in my mind. The formality of this commitment always seems to trigger an increase in small daily miracles.

Within a week, I had received several unsolicited phone calls about potential sales jobs. Then I was invited to interview with the UK division of a large French pharmaceutical company that was expanding its sales force. There was a vacancy right where I lived, and the salary plus benefits were enough to double our household income. The phone call came out of the blue, as a result of someone at the hospital recommending me to a sales manager they had met months earlier.

Family and friends warned me against taking the job. They said I had a secure position at the hospital and that in sales, people were let go all the time. They told me I was not cold and calculating enough in that dog-eat-dog world. Their fear for me was out of a genuine concern for our welfare, but I still needed to filter out that energy and choose my own reaction. I chose to follow the synchronicity that had just shown up, and I accepted the offer.

I started off as a trainee sales representative, which, despite the better salary, was something of a step back from the fancy title I had at the hospital. In many ways, the hospital position had been a cliff fall below where I was in the Royal Navy. In everyone's view I was going downhill fast, but I didn't see it that way. I was already aware of the way of the winding staircase in my life. That did not stop the criticism or gossip all around me, and I had to work hard to tune it out.

On the five-week training course, I stuck with my Taking Quiet Time discipline, and to my surprise found that I was a natural. Ideas, answers, and solutions all popped into my head when I needed them. More surprising was the fact that I found myself thoroughly enjoying the experience. The high integrity of my peers and bosses surprised me and completely changed my mental image of what a successful sales person is all about. These people really cared about the patients as much as their own success, and most had a medical background.

When I was let loose on my sales territory, I found that the customers I called on liked the fact I had experience of the hospital life, and appreciated that I knew the limitations of our drugs as much as the benefits. I discovered sales was not about "taking," as my father seemed to think, but about "giving," by satisfying customers and their needs.

I never looked back. I woke up every morning excited to go to work. Six months later, I was sunbathing in Spain after winning my first sales prize. Within a year I was in Nassau for a week, and the following year, I learned to ski in Switzerland. Travel was back on the agenda.

Within a few months, I was promoted to professional sales representative, and then to executive representative by the end of the first year. Taking quiet time was easier now because I had a company car. If it was too noisy at home, I would drive a half-mile to a quiet spot and find stillness for twenty minutes before driving on to my first sales call.

My regional manager was easy to work with, but he had been in the job many years, and he was counting his days to retirement. Great ideas for improving efficiency and success kept popping into my head, and unlike the hospital staff, he was receptive to it all, so long as I did the work to implement them. He came to rely on me to take any new recruits under my wing, and for the general organization of the region. I was promoted once more, to district manager.

At the end of 1988, less than eighteen months since I made the *commitment to change,* I was promoted a fourth time to regional manager in charge of a team of seven salespeople, all older than me. Next, I found I was being head-hunted by a progressive company, and I was able to instigate more bright ideas to improve our success as a team. At that company, a global conglomerate, I won manager of the year three years running. I enjoyed the recognition, but more than that, each prize came with an extra week's vacation and four thousand dollars in travel vouchers. My wife and I had some of our best travel adventures ever.

Then in 1991, I was the first sales manager ever to win the UK marketing professional of the year. The people in the marketing department were furious about the award, but their fury was born of embarrassment that none of them had even been nominated. Reluctantly, they attended a big awards ceremony in London when, with my mentality shield firmly in place, the corporate president presented me my prize on stage. There was a bronze statue and a sealed envelope. Given the multi-billion dollar profits made by the corporation, I felt sure that envelope held my financial freedom. In the privacy of a restroom cubicle, I nervously tore open the envelope and then stared in disbelief at my prize—a single share of stock (worth about ninety dollars). Rare is the person who gets rich working for someone else!

I introduced my early version of *Three Simple Steps* to the sales forces and watched with pride over the next years as many went on to enjoy similar success. In my experience of sharing this philosophy, I found most people readily accepted Steps One and Three but struggled with Step Two. It seemed possible to have some success by implementing part of the program, but I wonder how far they might have gone if they could have got over their discomfort at something as innocuous as taking quiet time for twenty minutes a day.

Success continued for me after moving to the United States in 1994; before long, I was enjoying the high life with a mid-six-figure salary, a job I enjoyed, and the sort of travel and adventure my wife and I had dreamed of in our courting days. Since seeing that look in Harry's eyes in 1983, I had done nothing more profound than add Step Two and Three to my life. The changes in my life were incredible. I had not acquired any new skill or talent or won the lottery, but people we knew thought I must have.

After seeing Harry in that state of near-homelessness, my siblings and I rallied for a few years to help rebuild his life and self-esteem, each doing their bit to try to keep the pretense of family unity. He found work as a taxi driver. Soon, he met a female passenger who had recently lost her husband to cancer. They bonded. She needed someone to care for, and he needed to be taken care of. He moved into her neat cottage and lived a normal life again with good food, clean clothes, and an endless supply of cigarettes.

Harry continued with his shady dealings, some of which required me to attend court to plead my innocence of fraud. Eventually, I had to make one of the hardest decisions of my life and switch that negative input off. Sometimes, it is the only solution, and I kept my communications with him to a minimum from then on.

His lifelong smoking finally caught up with him when he was diagnosed with esophageal cancer in 1995. He was admitted to hospital for surgery. I flew over from the United States. My sister was at his bedside and looked concerned when I walked onto the ward. She knew there was tension between us, but I simply kissed him on the forehead, and he greeted me with the same "Hello, Son" as when I encountered him in that hovel, and as if he had been expecting me all along.

He died in 1996. Three people attended his funeral: his girlfriend, his aunt, and one of his children. He is buried next to Audrey.

At the only funeral home in the nearest small town, my siblings were taking care of duties when the director said that he recognized the family name, and started turning pages in a dusty ledger. "I believe I arranged the burials for his father and mother many years ago," he said while scanning lists of the names of the deceased. He stopped on a page. "Ah, yes, here they are. George Frederick, 1971. Emily, 1976." He paused, peered over his spectacles, and made an embarrassed cough. "I'm afraid your father never paid for any of the funerals." It was fitting irony, and my siblings said they tried not to laugh as they handed over a credit card.

In 2000, I made a return trip to the United Kingdom, and met up with my brother and sister at the graveyard. Harry, Audrey, George, and Emily's graves all had a great view of the old farmhouse. After paying our respects, we crossed the fields and went to see what had become of the derelict home. It had been eighteen years since I last saw it. Shortly after Harry had been evicted, I took my wife-to-be out there to show her where I grew up. Within minutes, a local farmer, wielding a heavy hammer came charging at me while yelling, "We don't want your sort here anymore." My wife must have wondered what she was getting into and I had not been back since.

No one came to chase us off this time. Part of the roof had collapsed, and the outbuildings had turned to rubble, but it looked very much the same to me. My brother squeezed through an open window, and then appeared at the front door, pale with shock. Behind the door was a pile of final demand letters and unpaid invoices two feet high. Harry had left no forwarding address, and the owners had simply shut up the house and let it go to further ruin. No one thought to tell the mailman that no one was home.

The inside of the house resembled a ghost ship. The kitchen table was set for breakfast as if we had been transported back in time to 1982. Harry's bedroom was still made, the covers turned down as if he had just got up. Harry's bed gown lay across the duvet. In an airing closet, I found a pile of his shirts still ironed and neatly folded. None of us were prepared to find our home that way.

We walked around in a surreal silence, my sister unable to stop tears spilling down her cheeks, my brother and I just pointing and shaking our heads. Our old toys littered the playroom. Our bedrooms were as we left them, beds made up awaiting our return. The cot where Audrey had spent her last few days was still set up in the lounge. Beside the hearth were her slippers and mittens as if still warming.

I picked up some mementoes and pushed them into my coat pockets. One of Harry's ashtrays, Audrey's favorite snow globe that I gave her as a Christmas gift when I was eight. As I stepped outside, however, I placed them all back inside the door. For me, it was time for closure.

When I returned to the United States, I finally felt ready to start my own company. I recall the morning of my fortieth birthday. Something odd happens to every man on that day. The night before, the last of my thirty-ninth year, I had retired to bed as a young, fit, trim man. The next day, I woke up looking as if I was six months pregnant. How does that happen? Sometime in the night, a fat fairy casts a spell and there it is . . . middle-age girth. Its effect is to make us stop feeling invincible and start to think about our financial future.

Money had never been a goal of mine. Travel was my main aim, and the high salary and benefits I earned along the way was something of a bonus. Now I realized that I needed to apply the three simple steps to my financial independence.

The media and people in my environment were keen to accuse me of insanity for wanting to start a business during a recession. I made plenty of use of my mentality shield, and filtered out the television news. Still, I could not clarify in my mind what sort of business I wanted it to be.

I was thinking too hard, whereas stillness is the opposite of that effort and exactly what is needed to solve puzzles. It was my wife who told me to stop trying to work it out. "Keep taking quiet time," she reminded me, "and the answer will find you."

The more we struggle, the more we get stuck. This is true in any aspect of the application of these steps. We sometimes get caught up in trying to solve puzzles, when what we should do is plug into the matrix and relax. We don't need to know how something is going to work out. We simply need to send out the desire, and let life fill in the details.

My wife and I were leasing a home in Florida at the time and house-hunting during our weekends. The three simple steps apply to all aspects of our lives, and finding our dream home was something we had our hearts and minds set on.

One Saturday, we spent a few hours driving aimlessly around some neighborhoods. Tired, we decided to call it a day and head home. Admiring the setting sun, I missed my exit on the road, did a U-turn, and got completely lost. We found ourselves in a neighborhood that was not on our target list because we had assumed it to be out of our price range. Slowing down to admire some of the lovely homes, a front door opened, and the owner walked across her front yard to push a "For Sale by Owner" sign into the lawn at exactly the time I drove by the house.

An hour later, we had agreed on a price. It was a picture-perfect home and almost exactly what I had in my imagination. The couple who owned the house worked from home. The husband had lost his job, and they had decided that morning to sell up and move back to be nearer to their parents in North Carolina. The woman had just returned from a store with the newly purchased "For Sale" sign. The sale went through quickly, and the sellers were so kind they even threw a neighborhood welcome party for us before we had closed.

The house backed onto open water where dolphins played at sunset. For taking quiet time, I kayaked ten minutes across the shallow bay to a sandbar surrounded by mangroves. A nature preserve one mile away was a great place to charge up my connection to the matrix. It was there I made another commitment to change, this time to start my own company.

With my current company, I worked from home but commuted to the head office in Minnesota every couple of weeks. Bob, the CEO of the company, was trying hard to get me to relocate to Minneapolis. I liked the city and the people, but it was where we had spent our first winter in America. Neither of us had enough body hair to cope with it. So, this regular airline commute was a compromise.

Part of my role was to build sales and marketing teams to launch new pharmaceutical brands. I had to assess market potential.

That can be tricky when a drug is the first in its class, and no one really knows how doctors will respond. I had a positive track record of forecasting sales for four previous launches.

For the fifth launch, the company was excited. My experience warned me that most of the employees working on a project tend to buy into their own story. Everyone is so keen for the success upon which their jobs depend that some partial blindness to facts can creep into the culture. We had a classic situation brewing in Minnesota, with everyone believing the fifth launch would be the blockbuster to make everyone happy.

In a routine press release to shareholders, Bob had announced the market forecast for the new drug was a half billion dollars in its first year. On a difficult commute, I had to come up with a way of letting him know my estimate for the first year was for only $5 million in annual sales. There was nothing wrong with the drug, but I knew physicians would likely only use it in very severe cases of the disease it was designed to treat and that sales would take many years to approach the levels Bob expected.

When everyone else had left for home, I sat him down with a coffee and presented my numbers. He paled. I argued that the gap between our estimates was enormous, and even if I were slightly wrong, shareholders would be crushed. It was time for damage control and a concerted public relations effort to lower the street's expectations.

Bob believed his own numbers were the more accurate. He asked for evidence of my assumptions, and I had to admit that I was going more on instinct than facts. His information came from a paid consultant, but the consultant had just fed back to him what he thought the CEO wanted to hear. Bob added that if I could not achieve half a billion, then he could always find someone else who would.

I called my wife from my hotel later that evening. I was halfway through explaining how I felt about it all, when she cut me off in mid-rant. "You didn't take quiet time this morning, did you?" she accused. I explained how I had to get an early flight. "You should have gotten up earlier. That's what you tell everyone else to do." She added that when I take quiet time, I am always calm in a crisis and confident that whatever is happening is part of the way of the winding staircase. She was right, and I admitted it. From time to time, we all slip back into the old habits. This is why I say these three steps are simple but never easy.

I was booked into a chain-brand hotel in the city. No matter what part of the world you happen to be in, every room in this hotel chain looks the same. I usually stay in boutique hotels that at least have gardens or views so I can keep plugged into the matrix, but this trip had been arranged by someone else at short notice.

A few miles away was a Wellness Center, situated on the edge of the scenic Minnetonka wetlands. Primarily a spa in a serene setting, it offers nutritional and lifestyle guidance for people who want to lose weight and live healthier. The therapists take care of their clients without judgment and also work on the spiritual and energy disturbances they believe underlie a tendency toward obesity. It attracts people from all over the country and has uniquely styled bedrooms for those who choose to stay on site. Years before, I had learned that when all the rooms are not taken, they can be reserved by non-members, just like a hotel room. I had stayed there several times and found it a place to plug powerfully into the matrix. I used to take some good-natured ribbing from my peers about it.

I called and found a room was available. When I arrived, the place was just about shut down for the night. Other than the security guard, I appeared to have the building to myself.

The bedrooms are on the second story. At the end of the corridor is a staircase that winds up a tower to a meditation room. The spa believes meditation can help obese people in many healthful ways. The circular room has floor-to-ceiling windows, affording views over marshland. Before turning in for the night, I sat up there for a couple of hours. I reiterated my desire to start my own company and took quiet time a little late in the day.

I rose early and repeated my trip to the tower room. The spiraling climb reminded me that all good things in my life go the way of the winding staircase. Then I grabbed a healthy breakfast before heading back to the office.

The atmosphere in the office was tense. Word was out that Bob was mad with me. There is no such thing as winning an argument, especially with your boss. The Spanish have a lovely saying for this: "When someone argues with a fool, it is hard to tell the difference." Most people stayed clear of me, as if I had become contagious. I rechecked my market assumption. If anything, I felt I was being overly optimistic and even $5 million in annual sales would take a lot of effort. I looked for support from other executives but soon realized I was alone on this.

I went back to see Bob in his office. Neither of us held onto anger, and even in the heat of our battle, there was still a mutual respect present between us. I told him I accepted that he was in a difficult position. If he could not accept my forecast, I would step aside so he could find a replacement quickly. I offered to help that person with a transitional period because I still wanted the company to succeed. I was for their success, even if I could not be part of it. He accepted my resignation. We negotiated a fair settlement and an amicable parting.*

I felt the greatest peace, and the decision felt right intuitively. I got to the airport well ahead of my flight time. The Minneapolis

---

* To wrap up the story, the company went on to launch its fifth product. First-year sales amounted to just under $5 million. The company was sold three years later with the share price at its lowest since I first joined the company. As I was writing this, I checked the new company's SEC filings and saw that sales for the product after ten years on the market have reached nearly $170 million a year.

airport is a fine one if you have time on your hands. I had an unhealthy lunch to counterbalance the spa breakfast, then killed some time with window-shopping.

I was at the foot of an escalator, just about to head up to the VIP lounge, when the idea for the perfect business hit me. It just popped into my head. It was not a single thread or a vague notion. The whole concept flashed into my mind. It seemed so obvious that I wanted to hit myself for not coming up with it sooner. I remember laughing out loud and receiving puzzled looks from strangers standing around me. These moments of insight happen all the time when you practice the three steps in this book and are a thrilling experience every time.

Immediately to my right was a small bookstore. Something drew me to it. In the business section was a single copy of a book, so small that I was surprised it had not fallen behind a shelf. It was about why many small businesses fail within a year. I bought the only copy and devoured it on the flight home.

I was fired up when I landed. I had sketched out a business plan on the back of a napkin. The business model had never been attempted before in my industry. I needed to raise investment, but had no connections in that world. I also needed to convince my ex-CEO, the one I just fell out with, to let me purchase one of the company's assets.

I never ask how something can be achieved. I set the target and let life fill in the details. On the drive home from the airport, I tried to work out how to explain all of this to my wife. I planned a dinner and rehearsed what I would say. We would need to sell our dream home, which we had only been living in for a short while. As I entered the house, she took one look at me and said, "You're starting your own business!" She is always a step ahead of me. A little abashed, I mumbled about maybe having to sell the house. "Okay," she said. "Now, what do you fancy for dinner?"

Through dinner, we talked about the idea, the structure, and what I wanted to achieve for patients. We both got fired up, and it was well into the early hours before we retired to bed.

■ ■ ■

This concludes Step Two. When I have taught these principles to individuals and groups, I usually find that they readily adopt Step One and Three. In those steps, it is very easy to connect the dots between something good showing up in their lives, and a change they made in their mentality or goal setting. It is harder to trace the link between taking quiet time and reconnecting with nature, and the great idea that just popped into your head while you were changing the oil in the car. It takes time to re-wire those neurons, and it takes time for your mentality to be sufficiently under control for the ideas to surface with the energy required to get a reaction from you. Stick with Step Two, and you'll never regret it.

I can only encourage you to make this Step Two a consistent part of a new routine. Not even my closest family and friends knew I did this, but it has catapulted my adventure forward. Other people who have done this consistently tell me it has changed their lives just as dramatically and permanently for the better.

I do understand the challenges of trying to form new habits, especially when I am encouraging individualism. There is no peer group pressure to make you stick to it. Please do use www .threesimplesteps.com as a helping hand. Consider it the peer support group for those times when you need a little encouragement. We all need it from time to time.

Step Three is all about turning those great ideas into your real-life experiences. This is when it starts to get really exciting. This is when we allow ourselves to be the magicians we were born to be. Enjoy.

PART THREE

BEYOND THE QUICKSAND

3

Transforming Ideas into Achievements

$$E = MC^2$$

ALBERT EINSTEIN

Therefore also: M = E/C²

where: M *is mass (or material),* E *is energy (or thought), and*
C *is the speed of light in a vacuum (or nothingness).*
The higher the E, the bigger the M.

INSTEIN'S PHYSICAL LAW THAT says energy and matter are equivalents of each other and interchangeable is a clue to the secret of success; it explains how to turn intangible ideas into real things. This conversion of thought energy into things should not be a secret because it is a proven law of physics, but we tend to think of these laws as applying to nature around us, excluding ourselves from our definition of nature. We are, however, made of the same stuff as a plant or the soil. As part of nature, we are subject to its laws as much as a tree or an animal, and $E=MC^2$ applies as surely to us as to anything else.

After centuries of suppressing intuition in favor of intellectual analysis, most people have unknowingly dammed the natural flow of this equation. This third step is about releasing that conversion process in our lives. With all doubt removed from the process, our minds would be in what I call a *state of knowing*. This is the state of mind we need in order to turn our new, great ideas into reality, and it is what we will work on achieving in Step Three.

If you were a seed, you would not be given to complicating things by analyzing why you are a seed and worrying daily about how you are going to get sufficient nutrients from the soil and the air to be converted into the tree you secretly desire to be. You would simply be in a state of knowing that you will grow, strengthen, and eventually become a tree.

It sounds like magic because nature is magic. Nature is the conversion of one state into another state. The occultist Aleister Crowley defined magic as "the science and art of causing change to occur in conformity with will." Crowley claimed that "it is theoretically possible to cause in any object any change of which that object is capable by nature." So, we can plant a seed and, with careful nurturing, help it bloom into a flower. We could also throw some inert ingredients into a bowl, mix them up, and heat them for an hour, then enjoy the magical taste of a freshly baked cake.

Crowley saw magic also as "the essential method for a person to reach true understanding of the self, and to act according to one's true will, which is the reconciliation between free will and destiny."

You need be neither a scientific genius nor a mystic to create something from nothing. Einstein and Crowley were obsessed with the why and how of the process of creation. They were both intellectual analysts. If we presented them with a television set, they surely would study the science of fluorescence. You simply need to know how to use it.

But because so few people today remember that they can create something from nothing, those who do are revered, worshipped, or feared. The truth is that everyone can do it, and it takes you no more effort than it takes a sage, but don't expect the sage to admit that.

7

A Matter of Knowing

LYNDA HAD LIVED WITH a damaged heart since birth, and at age nine, in 1967, open-heart surgery was the last option for her survival. It was pioneering surgery back then, and her parents were prepared for the worst. Prior to the ride down to surgery, Lynda took her father's shaking hand and, as he told the story for many years after, said, "You have no need to worry, Daddy; I intend to live a long life."

The surgery lasted ten hours. Fearing she could not survive much more time on the operating table, the doctors closed her wounds before everything could be fully repaired. They warned her parents that because of the incompleteness of the procedure, Lynda's chances of living beyond a few years more were slim.

Her mother had to choose between letting her daughter live like a normal child, and possibly dying from the exertion, or wrapping her daughter in blankets to try to extend her life as long as possible. Lynda made the decision for her. Not only did she defy the statistics by surviving, she lived life to the fullest. She played soccer with her dad and rode horses with her sister. She made the school basketball team and was the lead scorer every year. As a teenager, she went to crowded concerts and soccer stadiums and danced at discos like any normal girl in the 1970s.

Every so often, though, her heart did fail to keep pace with her spirit. After a fit of fainting, she would be prescribed bed rest that often lasted weeks and interfered with her schooling. Despite missing much of her basic education, she told everyone that she wanted to be a nurse when she grew up. Fearing her interrupted schooling would lead to disappointment, people tried to talk her out of it.

She responded by telling them that not only would she be a nurse, she would be a great one, specializing in cancer care. Then, she said, she wanted to move to America. No one knew for certain where her fascination for all things American came from. Her father was a cargo ship captain and often traveled to the southern states and Pacific Northwest. No doubt his tales had an impact, but she was also addicted to American television shows that became cult classics in the United Kingdom. She loved the Beach Boys' music and their vivid imagery of sunshine and sandy beaches. Her dad formed a strong friendship with a Texan. So taken was he with Lynda's story and her love of the United States that he sent her regular gifts of football uniforms and Texas fashions. Lynda was the only girl in her town that owned a selection of LSU sweatshirts.

During her teens, she volunteered at local hospitals and helped out at a home for mentally challenged children. This work further inspired her desire to be a nurse and increased her belief that she could be a good one.

Lynda scraped through her final high school exams, then jumped at the first opportunity to go on to nursing school. She proved to be a gifted nurse and soon achieved her intention of specializing in the care of cancer patients at a city teaching hospital. Nursing meant working crazy shifts, including nights. She struggled to sleep during the day, and after prolonged spells on the wards, she would often suffer health setbacks due to an exhausted body that did not get enough oxygenated blood from her heart.

Her heart constantly struggled to keep up with her spirit. By her midtwenties, it was enlarged and the shape of a football. The normal electrical conductivity that manages heart rhythm was challenged. She would suffer arrhythmias that, in the opinion of her cardiologist, were life threatening. Everyone cautioned her to slow down.

Instead she got married . . . to me and started her new life as a working wife. Within a year, we tried for a family. After several traumatic miscarriages, the doctors advised us that, given her heart condition, further attempts could be fatal.

Some of you reading this will know the pain and trauma that goes with this kind of news. No matter how much he may care, no man can fully understand what a woman feels like when she has been denied motherhood. All he can do is to be there for her. Friends and family were well-meaning but of little help because everyone knew about her heart condition. There was a sort of "well, at least she is still alive" mentality.

The media also has little empathy for a childless woman because the situation cannot be used to sell anything. Whether it is a comedy or a drama, whenever the subject is about trying for a family, the plot always ends with a joyful success followed by commercials for diapers or baby food. At certain times of the day, advertisements for baby-related merchandise flood the screen. To protect her mentality, Lynda and I became as proficient as gunslingers at grabbing the remote control and hitting the channel change button.

The hospital had a group for couples going through similar difficulties. Although invited, Lynda attended just one meeting simply because everyone was *against* their situations. No one wanted to get out of the quicksand and be *for* something better.

Later, we learned that of eight couples in the group, no relationship survived the trauma of this experience.

Lynda and I loved to cook and made an effort to eat together as often as our jobs allowed. We would sit at the kitchen table for hours and Lynda would talk about her longing to move to America. Since learning she could not have children, the desire had intensified.

The year was 1990, and we agreed that a fresh start was just what she needed. We were thirty years old, with excellent jobs, and a good lifestyle. Making the decision to move to America was like slamming on the brakes of a car halfway through a journey between two towns at either end of a straight road, then turning off the road to drive into the unpaved landscape.

Most of our friends and family said we were crazy. They pointed out how much we loved England, that I had a fast-tracked career traveling all over Europe, and that I was earning enough for Lynda to quit work if she wanted. They talked up our new house, the high-end company car, and our holidays abroad. The criticism was intense, but we were both comfortable using our mentality shields by then and didn't let the negative comments affect our plans.

We met with an attorney who was an expert at immigration matters. He struggled to hold back a smile while telling us that we had no trades that were valued in America, and that there was no shortage of sales managers or nurses. The minimum educational requirement for a visa at that time was two degrees, with the second being a higher qualification. Neither of us qualified, and the attorney said it was an impossible dream. America needed software and information technology experts and, at that time, we did not even own a computer.

When we stepped outside his office, we looked at each other and burst out laughing. Lynda said, "I have no idea how, but I just know we are going to do it."

I felt the same way. "Let life fill in the details," I said, using one of my catchphrases that annoyed everyone but us.

A few months later, I received an unexpected phone call one evening; it was an old colleague, offering me a new job. The position was with the European life-sciences branch of 3M, the global conglomerate based in Minnesota. We could sense "life filling in some of the details."

The new job doubled our household income. Lynda reduced her shifts and started to take better care of her health. She could have retired from work, but she loved nursing and was now fortunate enough to choose her own schedule.

In late 1990, 3M started a new program to encourage fast-track managers to expand their knowledge of other areas of the business. They agreed to pay half the cost of tuition for a Master of Business Administration degree, which was exactly what we needed to qualify for the visa to work in America. Although I had not been in a learning environment for years, I recognized the significance of this opportunity and begged my bosses for a place in the program.

Day and night, every weekend, and during vacations, I studied for three years on top of my regular job while Lynda helped me with crib notes and mock tests. One of the subjects in the course that fascinated me was the practice of Kaizen, the Japanese word for *improvement* or *change for the better*. It refers to the philosophy of a focus upon continuous improvement of processes in manufacturing, engineering, and business management. It empowers employees to take responsibility for improvement in their role and function, releasing management to focus on strategy rather than employee management. I championed its introduction in the European division with some success.

Unexpectedly, my boss left the company and was replaced by Steve, an employee from the Minneapolis office. It was his first assignment abroad. Before long, Steve saw the benefits of the Kaizen program and felt it could transfer across the Atlantic.

Soon, I was on a plane to Minnesota to present the program to senior executives at corporate headquarters. When I checked into my hotel in Minneapolis, there was a curt message inform-ing me that the meeting had been cancelled. No reason or apol-ogy was given. I was stranded . . . somewhere on the winding staircase, thousands of miles from home, jet-lagged and con-fused.

It would have been easy to jump back down off the winding staircase and give up, but Lynda felt that this was all happening for a reason. The synchronicity of the change in job to an American company, the MBA opportunity, and then the arrival of Steve were obvious signs of life filling in the details to get us our goal. Things are not always so obvious, so she encouraged me not to give up, and asked, "How do they know you got their message that the meeting was cancelled? You might as well show up. Who knows what will happen if you do?" With my resolve strengthened, I took a taxi to the corporate campus.

The receptionist was embarrassed and apologetic when I showed up. Feigning disappointment, I asked if I could at least drop off the presentation slides with someone in marketing. The marketing vice president had no idea who this strange Englishman was but graciously accepted the five-minute sum-mary of the material. As I was leaving, I asked her who else would be interested in what I had to say, a sales skill I had often used in my career. People like to be liked, and giving them an opportunity to be helpful usually works. She introduced me to another vice president in a neighboring office. Two hours later, I had met all the senior operational executives in the corporate office, except the person who had cancelled the meeting.

A few weeks later, Steve invited us to dinner. By now, he was aware of our desire to emigrate and the challenges we had to overcome. He had become an advocate for the goal. Steve told us that a new position had been created in America, and the executives to whom I had pitched my program were intrigued by its relevance. Steve had made a strong recommendation.

After another plane ride, I was offered the job, and when I accepted it, it was just two weeks after I was awarded my MBA in November 1993.

In January 1994, we relocated to our new life in America and our first experience of a -40°F wind chill outside the Minneapolis airport. Even the cold could not wipe the grin off Lynda's face.

8

Creating The State Of Knowing

THE THREE LEVELS OF SUCCESS

IN MY EXPERIENCE, AFTER many years of studying and teaching goal-setting techniques to eager sales and marketing people, as well as practicing the three simple steps, it seems to me that there are three levels of emotion that attract success.

The first level is *desire*. Desiring something creates a powerful energy that can magnetically attract better things into our life. Desire, however, is often vague. We may desire a better life or a different job without being sure what that would look like specifically. I often hear people state that they want more money or a nicer house. Because of the lack of specifications, we might not get exactly what we deserve and are capable of, but we'll get a better set of experiences. When those arrive, we feel a sense of relief that life is finally looking up.

Then there is *belief*. The more we understand something, the more we start to believe in it. Many goal-setting techniques recommend baby-step goals, with the thought that as we achieve each one, we build confidence in ourselves and our goals, which leads to greater belief. I often see this play out in the workplace. When people get promoted, it is not normally a surprise to them. They believed it was coming because they became so familiar with the role and their suitability for it over time and with their proximity to it. In most cases, however, the person who was promoted was just as capable of doing that job the day they joined the company. They just did not believe it. As belief grows, we get excited and our stomach twitters with anticipation. Belief brings wonderful new experiences into our lives, and when they arrive we feel like celebrating.

Finally, there is *a sense of knowing*. This is an exponentially higher emotional energy level that comes when we are familiar with all the specifications, feelings, and senses of the object of desire. There is no excitement because there is no doubt about its attainment. The removal of doubt comes about because we have clarity in the detail of what it is we want. This level of emotion can be felt in the many things we take for granted in our lives. For instance, I am so familiar with making crème brûlée from a certain recipe that I have a complete sense of knowing it will always turn out great, so the compliments I get are expected. *Simple.* When those creations turn up in our life, we simply acknowledge them with a quiet sense of gratitude.

Step Three is about taking something we have never had or done, something we have little familiarity with but would create in our lives if there were no impediments to its attainment whatsoever, and creating a sense of knowing about its attainment. That is magic. That is the three simple steps in action.

Traditionally taught goal-setting techniques can be effective at raising our levels of emotion from desire to belief. That will definitely help you pull yourself out of the quicksand and improve your quality of life. I do not believe that it is sufficient for achieving the American dream. You need to get nearer to the state of knowing, and the process of setting intentions rather than goals achieves that.

THE DIFFERENCE BETWEEN GOALS AND INTENTIONS

A goal is something we do not have that we aim to get. Our understanding is that the desired object or experience is separate from us. Traditional goal-setting techniques show us how to creep toward the object in baby-step goals, each step meant to build up our confidence until desire turns into belief.

An intention is a goal but with all doubt about its attainment removed. Baby steps are not needed because there is no doubt about getting what we desire. Instead of creeping toward it, we can simply sit back and let it come running to us. The main difference, therefore, between intentions and goals is direction of effort. With goals, we push energy toward the object. With intentions, we pull or attract the object to us.

This may seem like a subtle shift in mentality, but it is a critical one. Small changes in how we think make huge differences in outcome. Change a little, change a lot. So, as we shift our conceptual understanding from journeying toward a desired object to attracting it to us, we slip naturally into an understanding of the law of attraction.

INTENTIONS AND THE LAW OF ATTRACTION

Depending on their point of view, most family and friend observers of our move to America placed the credit (or blame) on me. They were able to see the connection between my job, company, and MBA. They may have heard the story of how I went to Minnesota and refused to fall off the winding staircase. None of them, however, have the insider knowledge to connect the dots back to Lynda's childhood intentions.

When I met Lynda, she had been dreaming about living in America for more than ten years. Enchanted by the space program and with a girlhood crush on Bobby Kennedy, her room was a shrine to all things American. She was already an avid New England Patriots fan at a time when no one in the United Kingdom knew the NFL existed. All her favorite television shows had freely rewired her mentality such that her speech was peppered with Americanisms.

She had already visited America twice on vacation and talked excitedly to me all the time about the positive things she found in the people and the country. After we were married and finally able to afford vacations, we went to America and toured both the East and West Coasts. She absolutely loved America, and the more she experienced it, the more she believed she would live there. It had long since ceased to be a goal she aimed for and had become something she intended wholeheartedly. To Lynda, it was just a matter of time before it happened, and that is why, when the attorney dismissed her dream as impossible, she simply laughed. By that point, she was in a state of knowing.

Before I met Lynda, I knew very little about America. I know this is hard for Americans to understand because, for many Americans, their own country is so vast they don't need or desire to learn about the world beyond their borders. Current affairs are mostly presented in local and regional contexts, which can create a perception that America is the center of the world, and everyone outside must be watching. America, however, only has 5 percent of the world's population. Europe has 7 percent, and my attention was firmly on that continent at the time.

I would have struggled to name more than a handful of states. I had no concept of America's size. The cultural images I had let enter my mentality were based on spaghetti Westerns I watched when I was a kid, and a few 1970s sitcoms I had seen on television. I knew nothing of American history nor had I ever heard of Thanksgiving, the Super Bowl, or peanut butter and jelly sandwiches.

I recognize in Lynda's story of emigration what no one else can, and that is that *I* was one of life's details in Lynda's intention. I was the vehicle by which she got to achieve the dream, and I was delighted and honored to be so. I turned up one day on her hospital ward, pushing one of her favorite patients in a wheelchair, and another of life's details clicked into place for her.

I had intentions of my own that were related to business and travel for which I had created equal emotional energy and was enjoying living them. I had been practicing the three simple steps for several years and enjoyed a life of travel and adventure, with a lucrative career. The biggest source of motivation for me, however, has never been money or recognition but simply to put a smile on Lynda's face. It is a priceless thing. I have been fortunate enough to achieve it many times, and so I set the intention of relocating to America. No occasion made me feel more grateful than when I saw her grinning from ear to ear as we stepped outside the arrivals terminal at the Minneapolis airport.

Depending on your starting place, the three simple steps can change your life for the better quickly or slowly. It depends how big your goal is and how much work life has to do to put the details together. Based on my new intention to put the brakes on my career and make a fresh start in another country and in a different job that had not yet been created, I knew life would have to start afresh to put all the synchronicity needed to work it out in place. I did not know how long it would take to make it happen, but I set out my new intentions and let life fill in the details. In three years, the intention was completed.

Like many women, throughout her life, Lynda has moments when she just *knows* something will come to fruition. She does not ask how. She will see something she wants and just decide that it will be added to her experience. When the intention is achieved and I ask her how she feels about it, she will say, "I just knew it would happen." When asked about why she moved to America, she answers, "I always knew I'd live here." For many years, I incorrectly called that ability *women's intuition* because most men have long lost touch with this capacity for *knowing*. We are in awe of it.

Psychologists suggest that women's intuition is nothing more than a heightened ability to interpret facial expressions and body language accurately, but that hardly explains how people can know without doubt about the future of a person or thing that has not yet shown up in their lives. It is not fatalism or psychic powers because we create our experiences as we go and according to our thoughts and reactions. I think it is more because history and cultural influences have rewired male and female neural pathways differently. This has caused men to lose touch with their creative power. Deep down, some women still know they are wizards. Most men today prefer to think of themselves as warriors.

WIZARDS VS. WARRIORS

Many books compare achievement to a warrior's journey. Being male and ex-military, I have always liked that analogy. I can easily imagine a castle with my sacks of treasure lying behind its walls. All I have to do is kill the dragon or two defending the castle, bring down the walls of resistance that hide my treasure, and claim my reward. The warrior expects those sorts of challenges along his path. Because the journey involves conquest and battle, the emotion of the warrior is often *against* something. So, for every successful warrior, dozens lie facedown along the path, having not made it.

Wizards, however, are those who can transform any object at will within nature's laws. They rarely have to journey anywhere in order to get what is desired. They live in a state of knowing that whatever they want can be attracted or created in response to their free will. No dragons have to die. No walls must be torn down. Wizards can simply create a new bag of treasure.

The way of the wizard is more in tune with nature's laws. While the warrior smashes his way through a castle wall to steal a baked cake from the kitchen, the wizard simply throws some ingredients together in a bowl and bakes his own cake. The latter is far easier and, so long as you have the right recipe and skills, more likely to result in fulfillment.

Another challenge with the warrior image today is that it is wrongly considered a masculine persona, one that includes hunting and fighting as skills to be revered. The analogy ignores the equally important weapons of intuition, compassion, and healing that are associated, also incorrectly, with the feminine.

Popular psychology suggests men are from Mars and women are from Venus. Certainly, we use different methods of mental processing, but at one time there was an equal balance of male–female energy in everyone. To survive, we all needed fine-tuned hunting skills to eat and powerful instincts to sense danger.

A shallow dive into anthropology provides ample evidence that men were once more praised for their powerful intuitions than for their fighting skills. In many societies, they were the source of shamanism, working intuitively with the spirit world to impact the physical experience and heal the sick.

Proof also exists that women were not the scantily clad "pot-stirrers" we see in Hollywood movies set in historic times. Semiramis from Nineveh shaped the Assyrian Empire. Boadicea, queen of the Brittonic-Iceni tribe in England, led an uprising against the better-equipped occupying forces of the Roman Empire. She took no prisoners and had no compassion for the invaders. In one battle alone, her tribe killed eighty thousand people. Queen Myrina led an army of thirty-three thousand female soldiers to defeat several male armies in Egypt and Syria. Rejecting marriage as oppression, they were free to mate with whomever they pleased. They were not women I would dare call pot-stirrers to their faces without risking becoming an ingredient in the pot!

Even in more recent times, there is plenty of evidence of women who have been as successful as men when it came to displays of fighting skills. It is estimated that 750 women disguised themselves as men and fought in the American Civil War. Tito's Resistance Army in Yugoslavia included more than one hundred thousand women, of whom two thousand were promoted to officer ranks. The Israeli Army included twelve thousand women who were combatants in the 1948 War of Independence.

The farther back in time we look, the more the evidence shows that in any society, males and females shared all tasks equally. Since men took control of education and especially the written word, a split in roles occurred. Men stopped relying on their intuition as they took their guidance from philosophical and religious texts, and then feared it in the women they tried to suppress with their new education. History books are filled with graphic details of what became of all that male insecurity.

Healers were accused of witchcraft, and women were forced into a subservient lifestyle, which still exists in most societies today. Education was withheld and religious instructions given to serve a male elitist agenda.

In Western society, things are changing toward a better balance but far too slowly . . . especially in America. When I arrived at my first management meeting in the United States in 1994, I was shocked to find that among fifty managers, only three were female. It is, therefore, no surprise that of the 1,011 billionaires in the world in 2010, men accounted for 665 of those with self-made fortunes (as opposed to inheritance). In stark contrast, only fourteen women on that year's *Forbes* World's Billionaires list have amassed personal fortunes of their own. It is time to address that imbalance.

The warrior's tool for success is goal setting via small steps that increase belief. The wizard's way to success is setting Intentions. The art of creating thought energy out of nothingness and turning it into something requires creativity rather than conquest.

This is great news for women who may already be more in tune with their creative sides, and perhaps they won't have as much remedial work to do to see the benefits of the three simple steps. Men need to eradicate many centuries of having their brains rewired the warrior way. By utilizing the three simple steps, men can create new neurons so that it now becomes more natural to create via the wizard's way. Those new neurons have none of their previously learned behaviors. Getting to a state of knowing can become a more common experience.

The skill uses natural laws like the law of attraction and the law of allowing. Those laws exist and work all around you, whether you believe in them or not. Belief is not a requirement for wizardry success.

BELIEVING IS NOT NECESSARY

Now hold onto your hats for what I am about to say. Every inspirational book I have ever read speaks to the power of belief. According to even the most well-known books, it is necessary to believe in something before it can be achieved. *Three Simple Steps* is based on a different fundamental philosophy.

The laws of nature exist whether you believe in them or not. Trust in the physical laws of the universe that have no choice but to turn your thoughts into real experiences and let life take care of the details. When you were in the quicksand, the negative thoughts you had every day became your entire life. At no point did you believe you would get more of what you didn't want just because you thought about not wanting it. It just happened to you because you did not understand the way it worked. The same is true in reverse. Positive thinking returns good things to your life whether you believe it or not. It just happens.

When you trust in the process, you become an enthusiastic creator. When you succeed a few times, belief replaces doubt and hope quite naturally, and you grow into an active creator. Eventually, belief is replaced by a sense of knowing that whatever you desire you can create, and you are a wizard with the ability to have anything you want any time you want, with a little focused imagination.

THE EVIDENCE FOR THE POWER OF GOAL SETTING . . . AND WHY IT'S WRONG

Most books use the same evidence to justify the benefits of goal setting. A famous study, performed at Yale in 1953, supposedly proved beyond doubt that goal setting is the secret to success. This study showed only 3 percent of surveyed graduates set goals. Twenty years later, it is said there was a follow-up survey. The results showed that the 3 percent had a higher net worth than the rest of the graduation class in total. Some self-help careers are based on this research.

It is a compelling story, but it is fiction. No such data exist. In 2008, a Yale research associate reported that, after a flurry of articles citing the study in publications as diverse as *Dental Economics* and *Success* magazine, she was prompted to undertake an exhaustive search of Yale alumni archives. She concluded: *We are quite confident that the study did not take place. We suspect it is a myth.*

When challenged by a well-known debunker organization,

self-help gurus who had written books based on this study were unable to produce evidence. One famous expert in the field of human potential who has based his career on the power of goal setting in the sales environment was quoted as saying: *Well if it is not true, it damn well should be.* What kind of advice is that?

There is, however, real and solid data in Dr. Lewis Terman's longitudinal investigation of 1,528 gifted children with IQs at the genius level. An American psychologist, Terman was a pioneer in educational psychology in the early twentieth century at the Stanford University School of Education. He is best known as the inventor of the Stanford-Binet IQ test. The objective was to gain a better understanding of the relationship between human intelligence and human achievement. It continued for decades and became world famous for its discovery that intelligence was the lesser of several factors that determined achievement.

Discipline and self-confidence were found to be more important than intelligence for achieving things. By far the most important factor, however, was a tendency to set goals.

I like that phraseology because a tendency is a habit. If your habitual reaction to a circumstance is to set a goal, then you can be sure you have mastered the three steps. Your mentality is so under control that your thoughts are about what you are for, and your habitual reaction is to launch an Intention to get it. As stated previously, an Intention is a goal with all doubt about its attainment removed. Intentions have three key properties.

PROPERTIES OF INTENTIONS: THE THREE P'S

1. Intentions Are *P*ast Tense.

Because the power of getting to a state of knowing is in the detailed understanding of the Intention, one of the tricks is to imagine yourself transported into the future, immediately after experiencing what you desire. That causes your mind to try to recollect what took place; that in turn increases the detail and familiarity with the desire . . . because you already achieved it. You experience in your imagination what it felt like to have that desire. Your mind automatically starts to fill in the detail of what it took to get there.

2. Intentions are *P*ositive.

Words have immense power, so keep them positive and with hyperbole. For instance, if being slim is an Intention, *I lose weight* would be the wrong way to word it because the word *weight* creates a negative thought and *losing* is an *against* emotion. More of it comes back to you. The more powerful use of words would be *I am fit, slim, and healthy. People have complimented me on my great figure.* Keep in mind the need for the Intention to be *for* something you want, and not *against* something you don't want.

3. Intentions are *P*ersonal.

Intentions cannot be used to interfere with other lives. They can only be for *you.* You can have responsibility and accountability only for your life experiences. The body, mind, and soul connection is too complicated for anyone currently living to comprehend, and we cannot assume that we know what is best for someone else. We don't know their purpose in this life, where they came from, or where they have to go to fulfill it.

Many years ago, I learned about a married couple who were excellent physicians and set a goal of getting their son through the best medical school. It consumed all their energy, but the son never wanted to be a doctor, and hadn't the courage to tell his parents. He became an excellent doctor but deep down was unhappy. He died of cancer in his thirties. Many years later, the son spoke through one of this country's most gifted mediums who did not know any of the family or their history. He explained that the internal conflict of having to do something that his parents intended, when he did not want it for himself, set up a physiological energy conflict that caused his illness.

Intentions are as powerful as a magic wand and we have to exercise caution in how we use them. They are in the first person such as *I have, I am, I won, I got.*

THE PROCESS FOR SETTING INTENTIONS

You selected a favorite, private place for the essential moment you made a commitment to change. A similar reverence is important when you set your Intentions.

I schedule one half-day, always in January, for setting my annual Intentions. I look forward to it all through the holiday season, because when one has these three simple steps down cold, every day can be like Christmas, and you are basically writing your own Christmas list for the coming year. I think of my pen like a magic wand.

I prioritize this yearly start-off meeting and monthly review meetings so that I am never tempted to skip the ritual. I take a pad and pen, but the most important provision I bring to the place is my imagination.

The process for setting Intentions is simple. It is the opposite of goal setting. In that technique you decide what you want, and then think about how to get it. With Intentions, doubt is removed.

You already have the result, and the process is about getting ready to receive the benefit, so the trick is to imagine you already received what it is you want. Imagination becomes the key element.

IMAGINATION IS THE KEY

Imagination is a preview of life's coming attractions.

ALBERT EINSTEIN

There is nothing I find more delightful than lying back to imagine what it feels like to achieve some dream. Daydreaming is my favorite personal pastime. When we were young, daydreaming was the most natural thing in our lives. Later, people told us it was a waste of time and that we needed to be more practical. Now, we need to go back to being a kid again. It is one of the secrets to success.

When I was poor, I imagined what it was like to have traveled abroad. When I was in debt through no fault of my own, I daydreamed about what it felt like to be a financially independent person who was free to choose what work I wanted to do. I imagined what it was like to have eaten in Michelin-starred restaurants in France and to stay in five-star hotels in Tuscany. I imagined the sounds of the ocean from my bedroom window and the new-car scent and roaring engine sound of my super car.

To speed up the time between imagining and experiencing, think about something as already achieved. That way you can walk yourself through the experience with the same detail as a regression under hypnosis. Because there is no difference between thought and matter, you can think in reverse, and analyze what steps and decisions got you that success.

Exaggeration in imagination also works wonders. Years ago, when my only means of transportation was a bicycle, I had to ride the seven miles to and from my place of work. Being the northwest of England, it was invariably raining.

While I was cycling, however, my mind was in a different place. I imagined I was piloting my motorboat across a sunny bay. The smells of the ocean and the feel of wind in my face as I looked out from the open bridge to my private island intoxicated my senses. My heart beat faster and, at the very least, it made the soaking commute more enjoyable.

Years later, I got to live the experience for real, and as I powered my boat across the bay in Sarasota, Florida, I had a sense of déjà vu because I had imagined it in such fine detail so many times.

In your special place, start by clearing away the energy cobwebs using the same technique we used for taking quiet time. Do the breathing and relaxation steps.

Start by taking yourself back to your happiest memory, one from any time period, but the one that stokes all your senses. We recall great detail about the things we remember most fondly. Relive it in your memory in as much detail as possible. Let it cover you in emotion and satisfaction. Use all your senses to bring back the smells, tastes, and joyful feelings of the event. This is just a practice exercise to fire up the correct neural pathway. A happy memory is usually something we would want to repeat again given the chance. So, the neural pathway that is energized by the recall is the one that can open us up to receive other things we want. Now, as the memory fades, let it slip away. Take a few deep breaths, and then ask yourself this question: *If money were no object, if absolutely nothing in the universe could prevent my success, and all I have to do is point my right index finger to the sky one time to receive my Intention instantly, what is it I really want?*

Lie back and let your mind wander and wonder. Do not attempt to work out how something could happen. Just imagine it has and enjoy some time immersed in that dream. What is it you would have if there were no impediments? Let your imagination soar because you are now in the act of creation as your neural pathway is correctly aligned. I want to suggest things you could be dreaming about, but I have no right to place my limitations on you. No one can restrain your dream. It is taking all my willpower to leave the keyboard alone, and let your own dream unfurl without guidance.

You may find the reality of your current situation tries to intrude. Do not get irritable. Smile and thank your ego for the reminder. Let the thoughts float away, and return to an even bigger dream.

Coming out of these dreams can be like waking from restful sleep. Often, reality hits quickly, and doubts are immediate. Don't worry about that because you don't need to believe at all. Energy does not need you to believe in its existence. At least now you have your dream and the universe is privy to it. Once you know what it is you would have if anything were possible, write it down. Here's an example:

> As you were sitting on a blanket in your favorite country spot, and you let your imagination break free, you realized that what you had always desired was to travel abroad. Being a good French language student, you promised yourself you would visit Paris in springtime, but then you started a family early and the dream never materialized. Now you have bills to pay and a college fund to think about. Yet deep down, you know that if money were no object and you could have anything you desire with a simple gesture, you'd transport yourself to Paris to practice speaking French.
>
> When you close your eyes, you can smell the rich baking from a corner patisserie, and hear the sounds of an accordion player

as you stroll along the banks of the Seine. People congratulate you on your command of the French language as you order coffee and rolls at the five-star restaurant in your hotel. You imagine falling onto the freshly made bed in a luxury hotel room, the shutters thrown wide for a view of the Eiffel Tower, the sounds of the busy streets below echoing through the room.

You open your eyes, and reality hits. You realize you'd need more cash than you have. You'd also need to do something with the house while you are gone. The trick is to write down your Intention before too many of those present-day thoughts destroy your enthusiasm.

You write down something like: *I live a life with complete freedom to travel. I flew first class to Paris, where I spent the spring in five-star luxury hotels, dining on gourmet food, and everyone complimented me on my fluent French.*

According to the three P's, it is written as already received. As you start to think again about the reality of your situation, you can break that main Intention down into four categories that are necessary to achieve this main one:

■ **Financial Intentions**

My first consideration with any Intention is to estimate how much money I would need to fulfill that dream. I know in my mind that if I had the money, I would not hesitate to create what I just dreamt about, so my first Intention is financial. I write it down, and I am quite specific. It has changed over time as one dream is achieved and replaced by another.

From my starting place to the achievement of an annual salary of $50,000 felt like a big jump, and I am not sure I really believed it at all. I just followed the plan and set the Intention. In less than a year, I was earning more than $50,000, and set myself the Intention of earning $330,000 a year.

It was a bit of a stretch, but so many great things were showing up in my life that I never doubted it would happen. Within a year, I was earning a six-figure salary, and it kept increasing until four years later I had surpassed the Intention. I barely noticed because I had already changed the Intention to a seven-figure number. By then, I knew that whatever I wrote down would show up when I was ready for it, and from a financial sense I moved to a state of knowing.

Achievement Intentions

Next, I analyze what aspects of the dream appealed so much. What made my pulse race? At different times, it has been an opportunity to travel, the delight of recognition by winning an award, being my own boss, or even writing a book that made a positive difference in the lives of others. I add several achievement Intentions that are related to the main dream.

Lifestyle Intentions

I like to add some Intentions around the lifestyle that turned me on in the dream. For instance, my dreams were usually in beautiful settings, and climate was obviously important to me. I might add that I live in a sunny climate, or the beautiful countryside of Tuscany, or on a pristine beach. It could be anything, and at different times I have had language, music, and artistic Intentions.

▣ Material Intentions

Then I consider the material things that were in my dream. They can be large and small. Was there a dream car or home? Perhaps you have always wanted to own a certain painting or a beach cottage?

I have intended things as diverse as cars, homes, media rooms, wines, art, and sports tickets. I usually have between six and ten Intentions for material things large and small. Having smaller Intentions mixed in with the larger ones adds to the fun, because there will be a lot of check marks to enjoy as they show up.

In our example of the desire to travel to Paris, the Intentions you write to get you to that main dream might be:

- ▣ I have two hundred thousand dollars in my checking account.
- ▣ I rented out my house for one year to perfect tenants for five thousand dollars a month.
- ▣ I traveled safely around Europe for that one year and spent spring in Paris.
- ▣ I traveled first-class and lived luxuriously all the way.
- ▣ I spoke French fluently and was complimented by the locals for my fine grasp of their language.

How quickly those Intentions come to you depends on how much you daydream, how often you are taking quiet time, and how well you control your positive mentality—in other words, how consistently you practice the three simple steps. There are useful additional techniques to help speed up the enjoyment of your Intentions, and raise your energy to the state of knowing.

THINK BIGGER THAN WHAT YOU REALLY DESIRE

If all you really wanted was to visit Paris one time in your life, you could set your Intentions around that. In my experience, however, there is a useful technique that can be used to bring your desire to you sooner. If you set your Intentions much larger than your core desire, you trigger several positive psychological benefits. By daydreaming and imagining a larger scenario, the core desire starts to feel more attainable. When it is about to show up, you tend to be more in a state of knowing, and you more easily accept the miracles that come.

For instance, when I lived in a cottage with a single rickety garage that was too small for an automobile, I had a desire for one particular automobile. The Intention I set was for a multi-car garage, with a different vehicle in each bay. When I eventually purchased that dream car, it was nestled in the middle bay of a seven-car garage. I was still as thrilled by the car, but not at all surprised to see it finally turn up. If a visit to Paris is your desire, set an Intention for a lengthy sabbatical in Europe, traveling around all the great cities. There is definitely a magic in thinking big.

THE MAGIC WAND: WRITE OUT INTENTIONS EVERY DAY

Think of your pen as a magic wand. Writing out your Intentions is a powerful way to speed things up. As you write, you imagine and focus, which sends out powerful thoughts and helps you create more detail in your imagination. It is such a fun way to spend five minutes. Write them on a pad, tear off the sheet, fold it up, and place it in a back pocket or a purse. Read it often during the day when no one is around to notice.

I like to do this every morning, and it is the first thing I do when I step into my office. My handwriting is awful these days, but that is irrelevant. It is the deliberate act of writing them that has the power because it fires up my imagination. Every time I imagine the dream as already having been achieved, I increase the detail. Detail makes it feel more familiar and that speeds up its journey to me.

Keep a whiteboard on a wall in a location where only you can see it. Intentions change regularly, and as each is achieved, it is erased and replaced, which is a wonderful feeling. Read it several times a day. I like to use different colors and change the wording regularly because the exercise makes me think more about them. My board hangs on the back of the office door.

Keep a written list of Intentions in your wallet or handbag. Have a file in your computer, tablet device, and phone. Never be far removed physically or mentally from your Intentions.

SPEAK INTENTIONS OUT LOUD

Speak out your Intentions when you exercise or when you are alone in nature. My dogs think I am nuts, but I can live with that.

IMAGINE INTENTIONS AFTER TAKING QUIET TIME

This is the mental imaging exercise I mentioned in Step Two. Sometimes, after taking quiet time, we can open the door to a world of chaos, and it can be hard to protect the new neural network in time before it is polluted. Immediately after taking quiet time, I pick one of the bigger Intentions and then daydream for a few minutes about what the achievement of it feels like. I pretend it just came to fruition, and then imagine the emotions and sensations of that. In effect, I imagine living a day with that Intention achieved.

Sometimes, I also read out loud a list of my Intentions immediately after taking quiet time. The purpose is to ensure that the newly rewired network gets an immediate positive dose of images to connect to before I put on my mentality shield and rejoin the world.

KEEP YOUR INTENTIONS PRIVATE

Never share your Intentions with anyone else. Nothing will drain your energy or weaken your creator spirit more quickly than hearing someone you care about laugh at them.

That, however, is not the only reason. Sharing goals or Intentions is one of the most common mistakes people make. While I was writing this segment, a perfect real-life example of why you should never share your Intentions literally walked through the door of my office.

To avoid a difficult home environment, Anne hangs out with a neighbor's family. The mother in this alternative family, Sue, is a nurturing spirit who has taken Anne under her protective wing. She is encouraging her to take charge of her destiny. No one cares more for Anne than Sue.

Anne has her heart set on a particular occupation. She interviewed for three positions and wanted one more than the others. Because I had encouraged her to use the Three P's, she announced that she had been imagining already receiving this job offer. I asked her a few questions, and clearly she had taken on board the advice about future-history. I was excited for her.

Unfortunately, in her excitement as the nurturer, Sue told me how much she had been imagining it for Anne as well. My stomach lurched a little. A few minutes later, Anne admitted that she had shared her Intentions with some friends. One friend sent her a text to say she had already purchased a celebration gift for Anne in anticipation of her success. My heart sank.

Let's use imagery to think through why her failure was almost guaranteed. After all, doesn't everyone just want the same thing, that good news for Anne? We now know that everything we are is energy. Everything around us is energy. Everyone's thoughts are energy.

Anne had an Intention. At the moment she had the thought, she was standing on the edge of a clear, still pond. The pond represents the infinity of nothingness. Her dream job is on the opposite bank, and all she needed was to find some way to send energy to it and have it connect. Once connection is made, the laws of nature fill in the details. The intended target must come to the requestor.

She picked up a pebble, which is the energy of her thoughts. The weight, shape, and balance of the pebble are unique to Anne because no two people have the same thought cocktail. She tossed it gently into the pool. Concentric ripples spilled out from the small splash and gently stretched across the pool. The outermost ripple moved toward the opposite bank. At this point, Anne was in complete control of her destiny. Soon the ripple would spill onto the opposite bank and the connection would have been completed.

All of a sudden, however, Anne's guardian and Anne's friends ran out of the woods to join her around the lake. Shouting encouragement like cheerleaders, they all picked up pebbles and tossed them into the water from various positions. Although they meant well, their pebbles are not only being thrown from different angles, but they have their own unique shapes, weights, and balances, which reflect their own mixture of thoughts.

The effect of their help was to send ripples out in all directions. Suddenly, there was a mass of competing energy in the pool. When energy waves collide, they become subject to what is called *interference*. Interference can be constructive or destructive, depending on the matching amplitude of the energy wave. To be constructive, the angles and amplitudes of the clashing energy waves must match perfectly.

Thoughts are as unique as fingerprints. No two people have identical thoughts and images at the same time. Anne's support is coming from different angles, and with different energy amplitudes, and that is more likely to cause destructive interference, even though the emotions are all positive.

Anne had lost control of *her* creative process. Ripples crashed into each other, and a mini-maelstrom was born in the center of the pond. No ripple made it to the other side. The connection was never made.

This is what usually happens when we share the energy of our Intentions with others. In reality, Anne can only have control over her own mentality and, therefore, her own energy. As much as Sue cares for her, Anne has no sense of how well her guardian angel controls her own mentality. Although Sue is shouting encouragement, she may also be so desperate for Anne to succeed that the actual thoughts and images she has are not of success but fear of what would happen if Anne was not offered the job.

Like all good mothers, she worries about Anne, and although the words from her mouth are gung-ho, the image in her mind might also be of how she will support Anne if the job offer is not forthcoming. Because we always get what we imagine, Sue is now as likely to get the experience of having to support a disappointed Anne as Anne is of getting the job offer. Their thoughts are competing even though their Intentions are noble.

204

When Anne and Sue left our home, my wife and I said together, "What a pity," because we knew the risk we all take when we enthusiastically share goals. A week later, Sue was in our house again and told us Anne did not get the offer she wanted.

Your life is at stake. Never share the energy of your Intentions with anyone. There are no exceptions to this rule. Even my wife of thirty years does not know what my Intentions are, and when I asked her about this rule, she told me that when she enters my office she deliberately avoids glancing at my whiteboard. She doesn't want her thought responses to interfere with my Intentions. Of course, we often talk with excitement about things we both want to experience together, but we do not know the specific Intentions that belong to the other person.

LIVING THE LIE WITH FUN

Many self-help books support their goal-setting programs with the practice of visualization. This is a technique involving focusing on positive mental images in order to achieve a particular goal. Because of the importance of making Intentions as something already achieved, it is necessary to change mindsets subtly when it comes to this practice.

Now you understand that when you have a thought, it has no option but to become physical reality. In essence, that means you can lie, and eventually the lie becomes your experience. In some ways, we have to become a bit like Walter Mitty, a fictional character in James Thurber's short story "The Secret Life of Walter Mitty," which eventually became a film starring Danny Kaye.

Mitty is a genteel man with a vivid fantasy life. In a few dozen paragraphs, he imagines himself a wartime pilot, an emergency-room surgeon, and a devil-may-care killer. Where he differs from the Walter Mitty in each of us is that, even in his heroic daydreams, he does not triumph. His fantasies always end abruptly and negatively. Our daydreams always end in achievement.

One excellent way to daydream is to imagine going through a perfect day. When I had little in the way of material rewards, I used to sit outside on a sunny day, close my eyes, and imagine how I was living my perfect life. I walked my mind around my dream home and garden, checked in on the super cars in the garage, helped my wife prepare a gourmet dinner, and then watched a great film on a huge media screen. All of these have shown up in my reality and are part of my typical routine today.

When I bought my first basic car, I imagined a Mercedes-Benz ornament protruding from the front of the hood as I was driving. At other times, I have imagined walking into a high-end auto dealership, laying cash on the desk, and driving off with the vehicle of my desires. I continued to imagine how it felt to be driving that vehicle, all the heads of passersby turning as I pressed the accelerator. I might drive it to a top-end hotel or a beach, depending on what fancies I had at the time. One day I got to do it for real, and it felt even better.

Additionally, I have daydreamed fantastic vacations, financial and business success, health, and relationships into reality. As I am writing this, I realize that everything in my life today was once a daydream. There is not one thing around me that did not originally germinate in my head.

Daydreaming is not enough. We have to add realistic detail by physically accessing the core of each dream. When I had nothing but a bicycle for transport, I went to the high-end showroom and sat in my dream car. I touched it, brushed my hands over the leather seats, closed the door, and breathed that wonderful new-car scent. At first, this takes courage because dealerships can be intimidating, but eventually you do it so many times that it becomes a habit. The fact you do not yet have the cash for a purchase is a minor inconvenience because you know it is on the way. The salespeople looked me up and down and assessed me as not being able to afford the car so they assumed I must be with someone else who could afford a car and always ignored me. Ironically, when the time came for me to purchase my first super car with cash, the salesperson looked me up and down, and again assessed me as being unable to afford the car, turned his back, and walked away.

At one time, my wife and I could not afford a vacation, but we visited the best hotels in the city where we lived, sat at one of the bars or in the lounge, and ordered coffee. It was all we could afford at the time, but we felt it essential to become comfortable with the environment and atmosphere that would be part of our future.

Initially, we felt like con artists. Being surrounded by the wealthy and successful took some getting used to. As you start seeing miracles show up daily, you will know it is just a matter of timing. The discomfort disappears when it becomes a habit.

I feel a bit nerdy writing this, and I hope it does not come across as bragging because that is the last emotion I could feel, but I want you to understand how far the three simple steps have brought me, and how they have turned an ordinary life into an extraordinary adventure.

When I first started setting Intentions and imagining success, I used to drive to the airport once a month and just hang around the ticketing area for an hour. I would read the departures board and imagine I was the one getting on the planes. Whereas others there may have been plane spotters, I just wanted to get so familiar with the environment that I felt I belonged to a life-style of travel. These days, most people are familiar with airports and travel is relatively cheap. What do you do, however, if one of your dreams is to travel only by private jet? Yes, a couple of years ago, before I sold my first company, I started hanging around those lounges too.

When we finally started taking vacations, we could only afford to stay in basic hotels. So, we spent at least one day of the vacation visiting the best hotels in the area and walking the grounds. We would also walk through the lobby and spend a few minutes soaking up the ambience. At first we felt like loiterers, but doing this helps add so much detail to the Intention that it speeds up the move to a state of knowing. Getting comfortable with your future environment brings it to you sooner. When we could finally afford to stay at the top places, they already seemed familiar to us, and we took it quite in stride because we had stayed there in our imaginations so many times.

If we had a small budget for a meal out, we would visit a top restaurant to share a cocktail at the bar rather than spend the same money on a full meal at a family restaurant chain. One has to live the future life now as much as budget allows. When flying economy class, we always took a stroll in first class, and took our time before going back to our seats.

Perhaps the most intimidating thing we started doing regularly was to make appointments with realtors to view multi-million dollar homes at a time when we could barely make the monthly rent on our little cottage. Again, it was important to touch everything, to sit in the media room, to test the temperature of the swimming pool, and take in the views.

Think of it as window-shopping. The objective is to live like a millionaire as often as you can but without the expense. This is a critical part of making Intentions into reality, and it is a lot of fun when you treat it as a game.

My wife was far better than I at this practice. She is used to window-shopping. I struggled at first to overcome my frustration at seeing something I wanted but knowing I could not yet afford it. When I realized I was just window-shopping for the future, I also started to relax and enjoy it. I continue to do it, except whereas I was once viewing expensive houses and cars, now I am looking at private islands and jets. What a blast!

TOOLS FOR WIZARDS

Successful wizards have certain characteristics, which I detail below.

Discipline

Discipline: *to train oneself to do something in a controlled and habitual way*

In more than twenty years in business practice, I have met very few people who understand the importance of discipline. Most confuse it with determination, which is the fixing of a purpose. Determination requires discipline, not the other way around. I have always been determined in that I intend things to happen, but I think it is my sense of discipline that has kept me on the right path.

Changing any behavior requires doing something different long enough for it to become a habit. Most people who start a new behavior fall back to what they have always done the moment a challenging or stressful situation appears. That is not a criticism, and I am no different from anyone else. It is a fact of life. I don't think we are born disciplined, but I know it is a characteristic that can be learned.

Our modern world provides lots of tools and devices that can help us be disciplined so that we stick with something until it becomes natural. The three simple steps require daily adherence. That sounds straightforward, but the challenge for us is that the methods are not hard at all. They take but a short time. They don't mentally confuse us, and we don't have to fight any battles. Consequently, our natural tendency is to postpone or skip them whenever something more challenging intrudes in our daily lives. The characteristic of discipline can help you avoid slipping up.

Skip them once, and the tendency to skip more often grows. Eventually, we forget them and go back to our old ways. Soon, we find ourselves back in the quicksand. Then we blame the techniques for our failure.

The way to become disciplined is to schedule everything like a formal business appointment . . . but with yourself. Set a time each day to take quiet time and try to make it the same time every day. Book your time in nature.

The way I have done this in my life is to imagine I am two people: the conscious person everyone interacts with and the subconscious person that only I know. When I make schedules, I imagine I am meeting with the hidden part of myself. That way I keep my personal growth formal and reverent and so avoid the temptation to lessen its priority.

For instance, taking a long walk in the country is such a simple thing that you would normally feel silly for scheduling it on your calendar. If you don't, however, that time may get allocated to some other task, most likely one that will not impact your ability to create success. You could put off the walk for another day, then another week, and then forget all about it. I schedule it with my subconscious self just like a business meeting.

Everything covered in the program needs to be a priority. From now on, the rest of your life must work around the three simple steps. So into your life add the tools of discipline such as whiteboards, calendars, and notepaper. You'll need to use them daily. Plus, you never know when those great ideas will pop into your head. I always have a scrap of paper and small pencil tucked away in a pocket.

Self-Interested

Most of you are probably familiar with the common warning given by airline attendants shortly before takeoff: "In the unlikely event of the cabin losing pressure, an oxygen mask will be released from the compartment above your head. Pull the oxygen mask to release the flow of oxygen, and place your own oxygen mask on your face *before* assisting others!"

Self-interest is placing one's own needs or desires above the needs or desires of others. It is in some ways alien to the way we humans have learned to behave. It certainly contradicts the selflessness recommended by many a self-help guru. I remind you though that most self-help gurus had not tasted success before writing about what it took to succeed.

As we have discussed, you can only control your own destiny, and this trip is a solo journey. Intentions can only be for you. You are in charge of your mentality control. You have to put taking quiet time above the needs of those around you. Whether they like it or not at the beginning, they will come to love you for it when the rewards show up.

Whenever two people interact, a connection occurs, and energy is transferred, flowing from the higher vibration to the lower. Whenever you encounter someone stuck in quicksand, energy can get sucked out of you quickly. We can all think of someone who leaves us mentally drained after we spend time in their company. I think of these people as energy vampires whose subconscious knows its host is in desperate need of an energy boost. Survival instincts kick in, and it sucks it from you. The person does not mean to steal from you. Nature obeys its laws.

Protection of energy drain starts with accepting responsibility for the current situation in your life. Blame sets up connections to those things, and anything you are against drains your energy. Being in debt is not the fault of the people who loaned you money. Being in a lousy job is not your company's fault. You chose to work there. Being overweight is not McDonald's fault for super-sizing. You chose to eat too many calories and not exercise enough. Simply accept it, start thinking only of those things you are for, and you'll switch off the energy drain.

Self-interest also requires an understanding that you cannot improve someone else's situation without them requesting your influence. It seems counterintuitive to the way we have been brought up, but we struggle to understand the needs of our own soul, so what right do we have to assume we understand what is best for someone else?

This raises the issue of the differences between Intentions and prayer. An internationally recognized spokesperson on the science of spirituality, Lynne McTaggart takes the ideas popularized in *What the Bleep Do We Know?* to explain that thought generates its own palpable energy, one that you can use to improve your own life.

In her book, *The Intention Experiment,* she summarizes the hundreds of prayer studies that show no positive correlation. In some cases, even a negative influence on the recipient of prayer was demonstrated. In a few studies, those prayed for had more post-operative complications than those not prayed for.

Formally studying the effect of prayer is fraught with complications in the first place, but she also shows that remote healing has been well studied with a 75 percent positive correlation.

One of the reasons for the difference in the results for prayer and remote healing may come down to the exchange of information between the person performing the prayer or healing and the recipient of the effort. When we pray, it is often in a somewhat vague way. Usually, we have scant knowledge of the person or situation being prayed for.

As a child I used to pray for my mother to get well, but because my family environment was one of denial, and open discussion about her illness forbidden, I had only a vague notion about her condition. I wasn't allowed to discuss it with her to gain greater understanding of what it felt like to have cancer. I was never able to imagine the cancer cells growing or the treatments destroying those cells. The detailed knowledge was missing which possibly made the ability to pray for her healing less effective.

Remote healing follows the rules of Intention setting. With Intentions, there is a high degree of detail. Using our imaginations and visualizations, we develop an intimate knowledge of that which we desire. In remote healing, there is usually considerable information exchanged between the parties with both having a detailed understanding of the desired outcome. These days, when I pray, I try to have detailed knowledge of what I am praying about.

A second reason for the poor results in the prayer studies may be that the person being prayed for often did not ask for help and was not aware that they were being prayed for. The opposite is true with remote healing. In that situation, the person wanting to be healed has usually asked for help and sought out a specific healer.

Unflappable

Keep your head when all about are losing theirs and blaming it on you.

Wizards are calm in a crisis, because they know the law of attraction means nothing will ever be sent their way that is beyond their ability to handle.

When I was a young, junior-level manager, I was intimidated in the presence of executive management. In the military, those at the top are usually there on merit. They are very good at what they do. In business, I wrongly assumed that was the case as well, and behaved with them the same way I would have if I were in the presence of an admiral.

Using the three simple steps, I found myself on a fast track up the corporate food chain. To my surprise, I soon discovered that many in leadership roles were not there because of any particular talent but more because they were golfing buddies with someone higher. I also discovered that many senior executives had not received any more training than the people they managed. Most people seemed to be making things up as they went along. One time, when I worked for a top biotechnology company, the vice president of marketing confessed to me how much he lived in fear of being found out. He had previously been an accountant and received no marketing training whatsoever. I was shocked because I thought of him as one of the best marketers I ever worked with and still do.

I often found myself in unfamiliar places and roles, faced with complicated data for which I had no training or experience. I realized that once the curtain is pulled back, most jobs have the same principles at their core. Each position requires a similar set of skills.

As a district sales manager, I worked with a handful of salespeople. As a regional sales manager, I managed a few district sales managers. As national sales director, seven regional managers reported in to me. As vice president, my team consisted of six directors. As CEO, I had an executive team of seven. The people changed, but my responsibility for handling a group of people remained the same. I didn't learn some insider secret along the way that magically transformed me into a CEO. I just did the same thing over and over but with a bigger budget and a fancier title. This allowed me to remain unflappable in any situation.

The majority of people want to be told what to do. If you have ever observed an accident, you probably noticed that most people stand around paralyzed by fear. One person, often the youngest or most inexperienced in the crowd, usually steps forward and gives orders to the rest, who are glad to be given something to do.

Thinking as an individual using the three simple steps, you need neither instruction nor praise. Others, however, believe they need both. When you find yourself catapulted up the corporate ladder, remember to tell people precisely what you need of them. When they do it well, praise them for it. You will always be respected and considered fair-minded.

The three simple steps can change your life so quickly and so dramatically that it is easy to feel overwhelmed. Keep in mind that life will not place you in a situation that can cause you harm and that there is a reason for everything that's happening to you. It is impossible to connect the dots when projecting into the future, but it is a blast when you connect them behind you as I have been doing in some of the stories in this book. Keep a calm head and all will be revealed.

Guilt-Free

Guilt is an affective state in which we experience conflict at having done something that we believe we should not have done or, conversely, having not done something we believe we should have done. It gives rise to a feeling that does not go away easily. It is like an elastic band that stretches tighter the farther you move from the quicksand. It feels like a nagging in the mind of "I want to, but I can't" or "I have to, but I don't want to."

Once you leave the madding crowd in the quicksand and begin this trip, you have to keep on walking. Do not even look over your shoulder. If someone behind you calls out, you might turn just as guilt is thrown your way. The moment you put out your hands to catch it, you'll find it attached to an elastic band. That elastic band will snap you back so fast that it will be a long time before you gain the strength to have another go at leaving. I made this mistake of catching guilt thrown by those around me so many times early on that I thought of changing my name to Bungee Boy.

Courage and discipline are required for us to step out of our comfort zone. What we do not often consider is that we also step outside the comfort zones of all the people around us. Our bravery forces them to review their own situation, which can make them feel insecure. Because they all tend toward security, they react in a way that can make you feel guilty. The people we most expect to support our decision tend to be the strongest throwers of guilt. This is usually a surprise when people first leave the quicksand and one of the main reasons people return to their old bad habits quickly.

Think of it like crabs in a bucket. All the crabs know they are trapped, but they still will not let go of the claw of the one crab that is trying to escape. Eventually, the crab trying to escape either loses a claw or falls back into the bucket. You must have the courage to keep on walking away while accepting that not everyone is ready or happy for you to leave. Send them good wishes, and focus on what you are *for*. To enjoy a life of advancement, you must become independent of other people's *good* opinion.

It also helps to remind yourself frequently that abundance is infinite. By wanting to make something of your life, you are not taking a larger slice of a finite pie. You are not depriving anyone else. Everything in the universe expands. Imagine how much money is in circulation in the world today compared to 100 years ago. Everything you create adds to the expansion. Adding to abundance is a natural law and free of any guilt.

On the back cover of their final issue [of the Whole Earth Catalog] was a photograph of an early morning country road, the kind you might find yourself hitchhiking on if you were so adventurous. Beneath it were the words: "Stay Hungry. Stay Foolish." It was their farewell message as they signed off. Stay Hungry. Stay Foolish. And I have always wished that for myself. And now, as you graduate to begin anew, I wish that for you. Stay Hungry. Stay Foolish. Thank you all very much.

STEVE JOBS, APPLE INC.

9

My Life of Intentions

ON THE FLIGHT HOME from Minnesota to Florida, which I took just hours after I had the idea for a great company of my own, I devoured a small book that discussed many of the reasons 50 percent of small companies fail within a few years. The most common cause seemed to be poor cash flow management. Having experienced such wastefulness of resources in my regular career up to then, this did not surprise me. My experience led me to believe in two maxims that had served me well:

1. Projects always take twice as long to complete as predicted, are twice as complicated as expected, and twice as expensive as budgeted. That probably sounds negative, but I have yet to find it challenged by reality.

2. One of the secrets for any business is to survive long enough to hit a home run. There will always be a good time in your industry if you can stay in it long enough to benefit.

Therefore, cash flow is a critical matter that can mean the difference between success and failure. Surveys of failed small businesses suggest up to 70 percent of closures are due to cash-flow issues. Fundamentally, there might be nothing wrong with the company, but demands for payment for supplies and infrastructure costs usually come before revenues are received from customers. Most of us have experienced desperately awaiting payday so we can pay some bills and go grocery shopping. As humans, we can survive a few days without cash. A small business cannot because lenders and suppliers have little empathy about the reasons behind a shortfall of cash.

I have always thought of a company as a living entity and cash as the blood that circulates through it. If it stops flowing, then the company, like any living thing, will die . . . and quickly. With the importance of proper cash flow management in mind, I sketched out my idea to build America's first completely outsourced, virtually run, pharmaceutical company. I still have the airline napkin with the original drawing.

Virtual infrastructure sounds like an oxymoron, but I had observed such wastefulness of human and monetary resources that I felt strongly there would be a competitive advantage to outsourcing. Reflecting on my career, I estimated more than half of my time had been spent in meeting rooms discussing things that had little to do with profit, performance, or customer satisfaction. I could debate as well as anyone in the room, but so little of it was constructive or beneficial.

Two recent egregious examples haunted me. The first was a company president's obsession with weekly staff meetings, which he announced spontaneously whenever it suited him. A collector of antique keys and bells, he would walk through the corridor like the Pied Piper while clanging an old school bell to call the staff to follow him to the boardroom. I was cajoled into attending my first staff meeting the day I joined that company, and I watched in stunned silence as forty people crammed into the tight space to spend two hours discussing the style of chairs to buy for the new boardroom being constructed.

I vowed never to attend another meeting, and I tried hard to point out to the president the cost of his folly in employee-hour wages, as well as the disruption they caused. They continued the entire time I was at the company, but I refused to join them. My absences were noted and became a bone of contention between us.

The second extreme moment of madness came when I sat in a room with eight highly paid vice presidents and their CEO, his two personal assistants, and the human resources director to spend a whole afternoon discussing whether the previous day's spotty attendance of employees during a storm could be taken as a "snow day" or had to be deducted as vacation. Everyone seemed to have a strong opinion on the matter and the room was split. I sat silently until the casting vote fell to me. I pointed out the folly and cost of the last few wasted hours. I would have caused less consternation if I had danced naked on the table.

Such waste of resources and energy in corporate America is commonplace, and I wanted no part of it for my own company. Perhaps because I was getting older, I had also noticed a shift in employee attitude from "what can I do for the company today" to "the company owes me and had better pay back or I am off elsewhere." Half the time, I felt like a priest hearing confession as I wasted hours soothing the bruised egos of employees who felt they were underappreciated and underpaid. Then I would waste a whole month of potential productivity while I wrote and edited performance appraisal forms to keep the human resources department happy.

There is a certain level of madness in corporate America that everyone just accepts . . . because that is the way things are done. The beauty of reinventing oneself and starting a new company is that one can put aside all that nonsense.

Most companies used short-term contracts to hire extra help when they needed it. I had done this myself when launching new products and was often a little embarrassed that the "add-on" company did a better job at their function than our own full-time departments. I noticed the employees of the out-sourced company came in and got the job done while our own people spent half their time surfing the Internet, talking to friends on the phone, or hanging out at the coffee machine.

One of the ideas that popped into my head was that I could make the add-on companies my dedicated business functions. By doing it that way, I did not need to build infrastructure or hire employees, a major cash savings and assistance to cash flow.

I saw many advantages. Because those companies had their own hierarchy of employees and abundant human resource systems to manage them, I could be freed up to concentrate on actually building the company and making it profitable. Cash flow management would be critical in the early phase, and with this concept of fee-for-service, I could manage the add-on services as demand dictated. That way I would not be saddled with unneeded overhead or idle employees, and the company could evolve in an organic manner.

Additionally, a small business cannot get away with excusing poor quality in any function just because it is small or cash is tight. It will not be in business long, and customers have no obligation to be empathetic. These outsourced companies were up to date with all the latest regulations and had highly sophisticated customer service centers.

I imagined this "hub and spoke" model not just as a diagram on a napkin but spent time imagining it working in practice. At home, I played out conversations and scenarios in my head, then imagined the delighted faces of customers who were actually able to call and get an answer to their question from an expert without having to go through the hell of an auto-attendant system. I wanted the company to be expert in every function but without the cost of building and training to that standard. As unconventional as it sounds, having a playful imagination is a critical part of the third step, and I imagined every part of the business model working together.

When I was sure about the model, I went into my office to write a new Intention for it. At the time, I had a list of ten Intentions that covered a variety of desires. Although exotic travel was still something that I enjoyed and wanted, I had added specific financial Intentions, as well as ones for personal growth, health, and lifestyle. Finally, at the bottom of my whiteboard was an Intention that had been there for several years that had to do with developing low-toxicity cancer treatments.

Although Audrey and most of the patients I came to care for when I worked in a hospital had handled their cancer with strength and stoicism, the side effects of the treatments robbed them of dignity. Sometimes I questioned which was worse, the disease or the treatment of it. I intended to do something about it, but I had not yet worked out what that was. It was simply a long-time desire that I had written and rewritten on my whiteboard more than a hundred times.

Then as I faced the excitement and nervousness of starting my first company, I added the new Intention: *I own a virtual pharmaceutical company that makes a positive difference in the lives of people suffering from rare diseases, and it is a huge success for everyone involved.*

There are many drugs that, in my opinion, are of dubious benefit to people's health. I was only interested in drugs that truly made a positive difference. Because the small number of patients involved cannot justify a return on the costs of research and development, the larger pharmaceutical companies often ignore people with rare diseases. There is nothing wrong or evil in that situation. It is simply a fact of life because the large companies have to answer to shareholders, and shareholders want profits. I believed my outsourced business model would be ideal to serve people with rare diseases.

Additionally, I had worked for companies in which the employees rarely shared in the success they helped to create. I wanted a company that rewarded everyone who contributed to its success, whether it was as a consultant or an investor. If everyone can see that their efforts make a difference, then share in the material success of it, it means that the company as a whole will be pulling together in the right direction. It sounds obvious, but how many companies are there out there in which the staff have to take a pay cut or get laid off while the CEO earns a multi-million-dollar bonus?

In the biographies of self-made men and women, they were not shy about describing how they imagined success before it arrived. Following his childhood dream of drawing comic strips, Walt Disney described how he was advised by an editor in Kansas City to give up drawing. Working out of an old garage, he befriended a mouse and began drawing his new friend as a cartoon character. He imagined a place where families could have fun together, where adults could connect with their inner children without feeling self-conscious. He idled away hours imagining the feel, scents, and delights of his theme park. Walt Disney described imagination as the key factor to success. I did exactly the same with my first company.

In a similar way, I imagined every aspect of my company working perfectly. I imagined finding happy, smiling investors, as well as seeing the satisfied smiles on the faces of patients who would finally have reason to hope. I also imagined my own financial success as a result of building and then selling the company to a larger entity for a multi-million-dollar profit. Even before I had started the company, I had a clear exit strategy.

Finding outsourcing vendors willing to be part of the new concept was relatively easy. Each worked in a competitive environment, and they could easily see that if they did an excellent job with a small company, it could become lucrative when the company grew. I was quick to point out all the household names that started as small, home-based businesses such as Microsoft, Apple, Mattel, and Hewlett-Packard. What better advertisement for the vendor than to be able to say one day, "We were there at the beginning and look where they are now." Through those telephone conversations and face-to-face meetings, I helped every vendor imagine success by painting pictures in their minds. Soon this business model became *our* business model and it was an exciting new approach in an industry crying out for change. I thought the business model innovative enough to garner investor attention, and set about putting together a simple business plan and slide presentation. I was convinced that, with my attention to cash flow management, investors would love it. They did not.

I had no contacts in the venture capital field and had never been directly involved in raising money for a company. I had enjoyed a successful career but had no experience with actually running or starting a company. These were limitations I had to keep out of my mentality, although potential investors and bank managers were quick to point them out. I was frequently told by investors and the media that banks were not lending money to small businesses. "The capital markets have dried up" was the chant sung by everyone I approached.

I followed all the tips and techniques as outlined in Step Three. I imagined successful meetings with investors. I pictured signing on the dotted line of an asset purchase agreement. I pumped my fists at the thought of getting the investment I needed.

As I traveled across the country seeking start-up financing, our household funds were running low. The travel costs alone made a severe dent in our savings. We decided to sell the house we had purchased just seven months earlier. Upon hearing that, everyone we knew tried to give us a hard time, but by then we had complete faith in our abilities to create whatever we desired and our mentality shields were firmly in place.

Within days, three couples made offers for our house, and a small bidding spree pushed the sale price to almost 20 percent higher than we had paid just a few months earlier. It was more than what the house was appraised at, but the final buyers lived on the same road and were buying it to move their parents closer. They were motivated to get it done quickly. We also cashed in our stocks and savings accounts.

Just as funds got scarily low, in April of 2002, the CEO of a company I had never heard of, one based in Seattle, called to ask if I was interested in coming to work for him. To this day, I have no idea how he got my contact details. When asked, he could not remember either. He attended a lot of scientific meetings and believed it must have been someone he met at one of the venues. I thanked him for his interest but explained I was starting my own company. He asked for a copy of the business plan.

A week later, he called to say he was intrigued by the business plan, and there might be a way to satisfy both our needs. He required someone with commercial experience to balance his executive team, which was made up mostly of scientists. If my business plan held up to scrutiny, his company might be able to invest in it and share the profits. It wasn't exactly what I thought I needed, but I was not going to ignore synchronicity when it slapped me so hard in my face.

A few days later, I found myself in Seattle and in the rain. The thought of leaving the sunshine of Florida for that climate was less than appealing to me. I met with the CEO, a man of high integrity with a persuasive argument for making the move. I was of two minds. On the one hand, the money would have been welcome. On the other hand, I felt if I took a job, it would be detrimental to starting my own company, and there was no guarantee that if I took the job, the company would invest in my plan.

Before returning home, I had dinner with the company's chairman, George Rathmann. He was honest with me. He liked my company plan, but he was not sure they could invest in it. We compromised. I agreed to work for them three days a week in return for being able to use their office as a base for building my company the other two days. If they invested in the company, their office space would become the head office; if not, then I could continue to use the office until I found investment elsewhere. The caveat to the quirky arrangement was moving from the sunshine of Florida to the rain of Seattle. It was a tough decision, and I was wavering. I returned to Florida.

While all this was going on, my wife had begun having heart problems again. It had been forty years since her open-heart surgery and the repairs were weakening. In the next two weeks, we made several visits to a cardiologist for tests. More surgery was suggested. The cardiologist believed the procedure would be tricky. He showed us a medical textbook. "This is written by the best heart valve surgeon in America," he said. "Unfortunately, she works in Seattle, but I used to work with her and could send an email to see if she recommends anyone locally."

We needed no other hints and accepted that life's details now meant we were to move to Seattle. My wife called the surgeon's coordinator the same day but couldn't get an appointment until about six months later. She made an appointment, but the next day the assistant called back to say there had been a cancellation and an appointment was available in two weeks. Within days, we had packed up, sent our furniture to storage, and drove with our dog across country.

In Seattle, we rented an apartment, and it was not long before the beauty of the Northwest cast its spell on us, as it does almost anyone who moves there. We have kept our main home there ever since and the cardiologist was as brilliant as predicted.

The biotechnology company I was helping out had been working on a research project for nine years but still had very little to show for it. A staff of fifty had spent millions of dollars but had not produced anything that could generate revenue. In the biotechnology industry, that is not unusual. Industry leaders claim it is the standard cost of doing research and development, and that is what contributes to the high prices of the few successful drugs that make it to the market. In reality, I find that many companies are led by scientists who strive to invent the perfect compound. Often, they don't appreciate that perfection is not necessary. Patients just want to feel better, and success can be achieved by something that is good enough to alleviate suffering. Other times, they strive for an invention without ever stopping to assess if there is an actual market need. In my opinion, it is never too early to have commercial input into a scientific team or project, but most companies bring commercial people into the development process far too late.

My role with the Seattle company was to find alternative promising drug development opportunities to license so that the company could show the investors at least some clinical or financial progress. The CEO also wanted his company to become the investor in my new venture. In return for investment, we would share revenues, which would lessen their reliance on further investor funding.

They had an advisory board made up of some of the leaders of the industry. I was not surprised to discover that two of them were oncologists who had once been presidents of the American Society of Clinical Oncology. That gave us a front row seat on every promising cancer drug development program in the country.

Within weeks, we had targeted several breakthrough inventions at the finest research institutions in the United States.

Soon, I had successfully negotiated a license to one portfolio of inventions and their issued patents. With no relevant scientific qualifications to offer, I found myself heading up a cancer drug development project. Although it was not yet a perfect match for my long-time Intention of finding low-toxicity cancer treatments, I could again recognize that life was filling in the details.

During this activity, the CEO and his board of directors declined to invest in my company. This way of the winding staircase was certainly proving interesting. I had no choice but to raise investment elsewhere, but at least I had the use of their office facilities. I preferred working from home, but the rented apartment was small and hot, and this arrangement was a good temporary solution. I was back on the road attempting to raise investment.

I stayed disciplined about the three simple steps, took my quiet time, and wrote out the same Intentions every day. Out of the blue, a man I had once worked with contacted me. He told me his company intended to take one of their small products off the market. The revenues were small and they did not think it worth their while to continue to manufacture it. His name was Don and he was distraught because he felt the product neutralized the severe side effects babies experienced when undergoing a special cancer treatment. Without it, the babies would suffer unnecessary pain and suffering. Don had heard through a network that I was planning to start a company and looking for products to acquire.

I was horrified that a company would make such a decision for financial reasons and agreed to meet Don. He was a vice president at the company and said he could help me work out a deal with the CEO.

However small the product revenue, I felt that having a real asset in the company would help me better demonstrate the effectiveness of the virtual structure to skeptical investors. Instead of having to imagine it, they could see it in action. Also, taking this risk showed I had skin in the game, which is something investors like to see. Finally, they would no longer see me as a would-be CEO but as a real CEO who was running a real company. I set an Intention for acquiring this product and used all the techniques to imagine a successful conclusion to the deal.

I was able to negotiate a fair price for the product. I only had enough inventory for a few more months, and I would need to arrange manufacturing for a new batch as soon as possible. I knew very little about drug manufacturing but was told manufacturing would cost three times as much money as I had.

At the biotechnology company in Seattle, I had just hired a drug-development director. Her background included extensive experience in overseeing manufacturing. She agreed to work for me for a few hours in her spare time to oversee manufacturing of a new batch of the drug for my company. The way of the winding staircase made sense again. I had an office, a potential asset, a manufacturing director, and a working business model.

I met with two people who had worked for me at a previous company, and they agreed to come in as partners in exchange for investment. The combined funds got the deal done and a new manufacturing run was completed. With an asset in the company, outside investors' attitudes were markedly different, and I felt confident of raising the extra funds needed for my real target, which was a product sitting on the shelves at my old employer. I had tried and failed several times to convince the CEO, Bob, to invest marketing support in that product. It was for a very rare disease, and before I left the company, only forty patients had been diagnosed and were using the therapy.

Revenue from the product was only a few hundred thousand dollars a year, which is a very small number by pharmaceutical industry standards. Yet, we had received more thank you letters from patients' parents and doctors for this ignored drug than all our other products together. The letters were a clue that there was a much greater need for the product. Over the years, I had done extensive market research in my attempts to convince Bob to invest resources. Just as he failed to believe my forecast for the market that caused our breakup, he never bought into my estimate that this small product could be a multi-million-dollar success.

When I called him up, Bob graciously agreed to hear my proposal to buy the product from his company. I flew out to meet with him, and he was open to the deal but clearly skeptical of my ability to run a company. I felt confident, however, that if I could raise the funds, I would have a deal for the product, and my company would take off.

Through a network, I was referred to a promising source of funding, a broker called Bill who happened to live in Florida, less than ten miles from where we had just relocated. Again, it was a pretty obvious message from life that I should follow this lead.

Much later, Bill told other people that he only met me for lunch as a favor to the person who referred him. He read none of the material I sent prior to the meeting. The capital markets were so dry that he "intended to pat him on the head, and then tell him to go get a real job doing what he knew. But I was just blown away by his passion!" Intrigued, Bill referred me to a private investor he had worked with before, and that meeting also went well.

With funding now seemingly possible, I needed to confirm that I had a deal with Bob. He took my proposal to the board of directors, but they turned the idea down. I improved my offer and pushed a second time. The better deal got their attention, and we reached a verbal agreement. Unfortunately, their board of directors was getting nervous about the company's disappointing sales progress and reliance on additional venture funding, and Bob was under intense pressure. One of the members of the board brought in an additional executive to shake things up. Bob remained in charge, but the friction between him and the new man, Mike, was palpable.

The deal was suddenly in doubt again. My calls to the company were not returned. On Christmas Day, I got a curt email from Mike informing me that the board had changed its mind about our agreement. Months later, I learned that this was a lie, and that Mike shared the same deal I had proposed with other companies in an attempt to get a slightly higher price. Fortunately for me, there were no other takers.

A few weeks later, I learned that Bob and his executive team were to attend an investor conference. Without an invitation to the event, I flew across the country the next day.

On the first day of the conference, I loitered in the lobby all day but never saw anyone from the old company. The next day, I skipped food and drink just in case they showed up in the reception area. At the end of the second day, exhausted, I went back to my hotel, and flopped on the bed fully clothed and a little deflated. For ten minutes, I lay there doing a breathing exercise in the same way as outlined in taking quiet time. It is a wonderful way to recharge those tired neurons. I got up and walked the mile back to the meeting venue.

The place appeared empty, and even the reception staff had left. I wandered around the various empty breakout rooms. A sign pointed to an upstairs meeting and I could hear muffled voices, so I climbed the stairs. At the corner on the first level, a door opened and out spilled Bob and Mike. We literally bumped into each other. This is how things happen when you follow the three simple steps, and as I recall this now, I remember not being at all surprised by it. In fact, I expected something like that.

There was an embarrassed silence. Bob said, "You went quiet on us, do we have a deal?" Caught in his obvious deceit, Mike blushed. I said, "I have been trying to get your confirmation. I have funds, I just need you to say yes to the deal." Bob shot a puzzled glance at Mike, and to save face, Mike quickly shook my hand and muttered, "Sorry, I thought someone had gotten back to you. Yes, we have a deal." He could not keep eye contact with me.

Within a couple of weeks, contracts were signed and money was exchanged. My dream company was up and running with two revenue-generating assets.

The first two years of business were bumpy and managing cash flow was as tricky as I'd foretold. The virtual model proved to be a savior. One partner sold out quickly. He made a decent profit on his investment. The other partner and I formed an indomitable team. Our investors proved to be very patient and supportive. By setting up a virtual structure that consisted of experienced and successful vendors, we created an extension of the mastermind principle that I had read about in many of the biographies. Although I was expert in none of the functions, each vendor was an expert in a specific field or service. They also had connections to other more experienced and successful clients from whom we could learn.

One of the most important lessons I picked up from all those biographies is that it is better to have a small share of a large pie than 100 percent of nothing. It is hard for many potential entrepreneurs to accept that they must exchange percentages of ownership for expert contribution or funding, but I never have an issue with that. The goal is to achieve a balanced team with everyone contributing and aiming for a common Intention. In this case, our Intention was to build a profitable company that made a positive difference in the lives and health of everyone it served. That became everyone's mantra, and the company mission, vision, values statement read:

Make a positive difference in the lives of people suffering from rare diseases, have fun while doing it, and share in the material rewards of a successful venture.

The letters we received from patients and doctors, who were ecstatic finally to have a solution for their problem, were worth all the effort and kept us all motivated. In a touch of irony, one of the letters received that second year captured what I believe the industry should be more about.

> Wow! Thank you so much for your medicine and service. It has changed all our lives, not only Becky's. You guys better be careful or people might start thinking pharmaceutical companies are really nice guys! I can't tell you how much I appreciate what you have done for us.

By the end of 2004, the virtual business model was a proven success. The investors were happy, and everyone who worked around the company began to enjoy the material rewards of their contribution to our success. By the end of 2005, we had expanded to provide five pharmaceutical products for different diseases and conditions.

During 2005, the Seattle biotechnology company that I had worked part-time for at the beginning folded. The investors had finally become weary of pouring in money without creating revenue. Because I had seen the exciting data coming out of the cancer drug program, especially the fact that the lead compounds had low toxicity, I made a substantial offer to them of five hundred thousand dollars to purchase the license. The money I offered would have allowed the company to keep the lights on for a few months more, and who knows, perhaps long enough to make the clinical breakthrough they and the investors were seeking.

George Rathmann had once given me another piece of sound advice: "When you are a small company and someone makes you a fair offer, take it. You never know if another one will come and the goal is to survive." The staff at the company he chaired was deaf to this advice. They spent so long discussing my offer that the doors closed before they came to a decision. It was like watching Emperor Nero play his fiddle while Rome burned.

A few weeks later, under the terms of the contract between the biotechnology company and the inventor, the license returned to the inventor's institution. I called the director of licensing at that institution, who was the same man I had built good rapport with during the original deal. I was ready to negotiate, but here's one of the golden rules of negotiation: *He who mentions a number first loses. Always.* I waited for his opening offer. Hesitantly, he asked for a fee of just seven thousand dollars. Within days, we had agreed and signed the contract.

Four hundred and ninety-three thousand dollars better off than I expected to be, I set up another virtual company called ANU.

ANU is an Irish Goddess of Plenty. In the beginning it was Anu who watered the first Oak tree Bile from the heavens and granted life to the earth. From the tree fell two acorns which Anu nurtured as her own, and in turn they became the God Dagda with the power to kill yet bring back to life and Brighid, Goddess of therapy.

I thought that was a good description of how chemotherapies aim to treat cancer. In killing the unwanted, they bring back life. Several of the compounds in this oncology program seemed to have excellent cancer-killing properties without the toxicity.

Having purchased the license, I set up a team of consulting scientists who were so enthusiastic about the promising compounds they worked for free. Under their guidance, we selected contract laboratories to perform the necessary testing, and I funded the costs myself. One sunny weekend morning, I treated myself to a glass of champagne as I placed a check mark against that long-time Intention for finding low-toxicity cancer treatments. When I connect the dots backward, I can see how the Intentions for my cancer compounds and the commercial company were achieved via the same move to Seattle, but all most of our friends and family see is that we are nomads who can never decide on a place to live.

For both companies, the next few years went very well, and I checked off Intention after Intention. Sales of our commercial entity grew significantly, and a company that boasted only $800,000 in revenue in 2004 was doing more than $15 million a year by 2008. All functions, including sales and marketing, were contracted as outsourced fee-for-service. We had no office facility and still had not hired a single employee. This model allowed us to increase and decrease services as demand dictated and proved to be highly profitable as compared to the traditional company model. More important, customers at the receiving end of any function experienced excellent quality service, and we saved many lives with the drugs that otherwise would not have been available.

The synchronicity in this story seems remarkable to those who do not yet follow the three simple steps, but it is commonplace for those who do. I can connect the dots retrospectively and easily understand how everything played out perfectly, but it would have been impossible to predict any of it. This is why I say that all you need to do is set an Intention, then relax and let life fill in the details. There is no point to trying to conquer the goal in the warrior's style by charging toward the treasure. For all you know, you could be running in the wrong direction. Be like a wizard. The Intention is your magic spell.

It has been hard to describe this story without mentioning by name the many fantastic people, whether investors, partners, scientists, or vendors, who contributed to the success of both companies. The story, however, is about how great ideas become reality through the use of the three simple steps. The story is about the process, not the people. I have shared my gratitude with each and every one privately. Many of us are still together in other adventures. In some, I am but one of life's details in their great Intentions. In others, they are details in mine. One of the most fantastic aspects of doing the three simple steps is experiencing the amazing people that show up to help you achieve an Intention. I enjoy that experience as much as any other.

In 2008, we expanded the commercial company internationally through the same outsource concept and soon children with rare diseases in Asia, Africa, and Europe were benefitting. We received letters of thanks from all over the world, and sometimes parents and doctors even sent us pictures of the people who had been helped.

Throughout this time, our approach was "whoever can benefit from our medicines gets access to them, regardless of their circumstances." As a result, we gave away medicine for free to about 25 percent of patients. That requires a very understanding group of investors and business people, and I felt we had a perfect team.

As time progressed, however, I felt the company was growing beyond the support capacity of the virtual model. I believe the virtual model is excellent for small businesses but becomes less efficient above a certain size. Our investors were split about the future direction for the company. One investor keenly wanted to expand, but further expansion would have required building a more traditional brick and mortar infrastructure. For six years, I had enjoyed not having to waste a month of my life conducting performance appraisals, and I had no desire to return to that life. It was clearly time for my Intention to be completed.

I think it important that any entrepreneur knows when he has done all he or she can do, and that it is time to step aside and let others take up the reins. Some people are best suited to maintenance tasks and some to construction. I am a wizard, a believer in the three simple steps, and enjoy starting things from nothing far more than I enjoy maintenance. I knew it was time for me to move on. I changed my Intention to: *I sold my company for more than $100 million in a deal that was of benefit to everyone involved.*

The first suitors turned up in late 2008. In early 2009, we accepted an offer to divest one of our products for $57 million, which was a terrific deal in difficult economic times. The purchaser went on to enjoy great success with the product, which in turn benefitted from their company's much larger sales force and resources.

Then we started receiving offers for the rest of the company. At one time in the process, there were 170 full-time employees, from five different companies, performing due diligence on our virtual company with its zero employees. No one but me seemed to get the irony.

We turned down better deals than the one we accepted. Of critical concern to us was that patients would be given the same or better care and attention in the future, and that was the case for the offer we accepted.

Eventually, the ideal new owners stepped up, and under their tutelage, I know the company will go from strength to strength. In the end, it was a perfect match. From starting with a few thousand, the total sales price was more than $107 million, just seven years later. Who says the American dream is dead?

In 2007, a trip to China had connected me with a billion-dollar company run by people whose goals in life are also to make positive differences in the lives of others. It is a remarkable company staffed by some of the brightest and most humble

236

people I have ever met, many of them Buddhists. For them, taking quiet time every day is natural. It is not considered esoteric but as normal as drinking water to quench a thirst.

By 2011, ANU grew to have several promising compounds in development, and I formed a joint venture with the Chinese company. I remain a hands-on director with the drug development program. Their much greater financial and people resources will speed up the progress of these promising treatments.

We agreed to name the leading cancer compound *AD1* after my mother, Audrey Dawick. Of everything the three simple steps have given me in an adventurous life to date, I am most grateful for this one small thing.

The End

Your work is going to fill a large part of your life, and the only way to be truly satisfied is to do what you believe is great work. And the only way to do great work is to love what you do. If you haven't found it yet, keep looking. Don't settle. As with all matters of the heart, you'll know when you find it. And, like any great relationship, it just gets better and better as the years roll on. So keep looking until you find it. Don't settle.

STEVE JOBS

CONCLUSION

IF MOST PEOPLE DO not read a book's introduction, I assume the same is true of its conclusion. I will keep it short.

I believe the application of these three simple steps can get you out of the quicksand and on your way to amazing adventures. Each principle is free and has no negative side effect. What do you have to lose by being selective with the media, avoiding the complainers, treating yourself to 2 percent of your day for stillness, and writing daily Intentions?

I look forward to hearing about all your adventures at www.threesimplesteps.com, most of which I am sure will be even more exciting than my own.

Cheers!
Trev

ACKNOWLEDGMENTS

Janet Wynne: From the days when we used to hit each other over the head with kitchen implements to today, you have been a constant in my life. Your support and encouragement has been appreciated more than I have ever said.

Edwin B. Hernandez: Who has been my fellow wizard for several projects over the last fifteen years. We have played, fought and celebrated like brothers during that time, and I can't imagine having anyone more talented or fun to create havoc with.

Sarah Maddison: For filling the void so readily and humbly, and for the best steak and kidney pie on the planet.

Eva and Gus: For stepping outside their comfort zones and pointing out the right path for me to take.

BenBella Books: Erin Kelley (editor) for bringing clarity and structure on paper to my cluttered thoughts. Glenn Yeffeth (CEO), a fellow re-inventor who immediately understood the significance of the *Three Simple Steps*. To them and the whole BenBella team who helped me to get over the discomfort of revealing personal stories, and who make the writing and production of a book a true partnership.

Papua and my spirit team for their magic. Sweet dreams to us all.

ABOUT THE AUTHOR

Author of *Three Simple Steps*, Trevor Blake is a serial entrepreneur. He was founder and CEO of QOL Medical LLC, a company focused on solutions for rare diseases, that he started in 2002 with a few thousand dollars. Its virtual business model was unique in an industry crying out for change, it was the top grossing nonemployer in the United States, and it sold in 2010 for over $100 million. In 2006 he founded ANU, a unique not-for-profit dedicated to developing low side-effect cancer drugs. In 2011 he co-founded Kalvi Medical LLC and is its CEO.

Prior to this, Trevor was VP Commercial Development at Ceptyr, and Director Commercial Development at Orphan Medical. He has worked in the UK, Europe, and the USA with companies such as Lipha, 3M, and Biogen and has won many industry awards, including marketing professional of the year.

A graduate of Britannia Royal Naval College (UK), he has a degree in radiography, and an MBA from Durham University (UK).

www.threesimplesteps.com
- Share your experiences
- Get support and advice
- Get updated content and information
- Request a signed copy

Want to connect with Trevor on how to redefine your life and find success? Contact him today! information@threesimplesteps.com

For a taste of Trevor's next book *Virtual Success*, which is a practical (but not dry) guide to starting, surviving, and succeeding with a virtual business, please visit his blog at http://trevorgblake.com where you will find many useful articles for success in business and life.